FIELD NOTES ON
LISTENING

Other Titles by Kit Dobson

All the Feels: Affect and Writings in Canada / Tous les sens: Affect et écritures au Canada (co-editor with Marie Carrière and Ursula Moser)

Dissonant Methods: Undoing Discipline in the Humanities Classroom (co-editor with Ada Jaarsma)

Malled: Deciphering Shopping in Canada

Producing Canadian Literature: Authors Speak on the Literary Marketplace (co-author with Smaro Kamboureli)

Transnational Canadas: Globalization and Anglo-Canadian Literature

Transnationalism, Activism, Art (co-editor with Áine McGlynn)

FIELD NOTES ON
LISTENING

KIT DOBSON

WOLSAK
& WYNN

Published by Wolsak and Wynn Publishers
280 James Street North
Hamilton, ON L8R2L3
www.wolsakandwynn.ca

Editor: Noelle Allen | Copy editor: Ashley Hisson
Cover and interior design: Jen Rawlinson
Cover image: Milky way over Bruce Peninsula stock photo by Filip Funk
Author photograph: Aubrey Jean Hanson
Typeset in Minion and Trebuchet
Printed by Brant Service Press Ltd., Brantford, Canada

The poem "Butterfly Bones: Sonnet Against Sonnets" is reprinted from Always Now (in three volumes) by Margaret Avison by permission of The Porcupine's Quill. © the estate of Margaret Avison, 2003.

Text from a. rawlings is reproduced with permission from the author.

From *Braiding Sweetgrass* by Robin Wall Kimmerer (Minneapolis: Milkweed Editions, 2013). Copyright © 2013 by Robin Wall Kimmerer. Reprinted with permission from Milkweed Editions. milkweed.org.

10 9 8 7 6 5 4 3 2 1

The publisher gratefully acknowledges the support of the Ontario Arts Council, the Canada Council for the Arts and the Government of Canada.

Library and Archives Canada Cataloguing in Publication

Title: Field notes on listening / Kit Dobson.
Names: Dobson, Kit, 1979- author.
Identifiers: Canadiana 20220159424 | ISBN 9781989496541 (softcover)
Subjects: LCGFT: Essays.
Classification: LCC PS8607.O25 F54 2022 | DDC C814/.6—dc23

The cyanide jar seals life, as sonnets move
towards final stiffness. Cased in a white glare
these specimens stare for peering boys, to prove
strange certainties. Plane dogsled and safari
assure continuing range. The sweep-net skill,
the patience, learning, leave all living stranger.
Insect – or poem – waits for the fix, the frill
precision can effect, brilliant with danger.
What law and wonder the museum spectres
bespeak is cryptic for the shivery wings,
the world cut-diamond-eyed, those eyes' reflectors,
or herbal grass, sunned motes, fierce listening.
Might sheened and rigid trophies strike men blind
like Adam's lexicon locked in the mind?

– Margaret Avison, "Butterfly Bones: Sonnet Against Sonnets"

CONTENTS

PRELUDE

The sound of snowmobiles blasting across the frozen surface of Sylvan Lake, Alberta, on New Year's Day.
The sound of fires raging across New South Wales, Australia, as streamed on the Internet.
The sound of drone strikes reported on the news.
The sound of snow falling on the blue and white spruces outside the window.
The sound of surface-to-surface and surface-to-air missiles.
The sound of a two-stroke, gas-powered leaf blower, which my neighbour uses to clear snow from his paths.
The sound of snow crunching underfoot.
The sound of a billion animals burnt to death.
The sound of three white-tailed deer walking down the path to the writing studio.
The sound of Donald Trump.
The sound of heavy ornamentation in baroque music.
The sound of an ermine darting in and out of a snowbank.
The sound of Brexit.
The sound of the ice in my eyelashes hitting the ice on my balaclava when I blink.

The sound of grief.

The sound of wine, conversation, a piano, artists sharing their work on a cold winter's night.

The sound of the seventy-fifth anniversary of the liberation of Auschwitz.

The sound of coronavirus.

The sound of the dog's claws on the melted and refrozen snow.

The sound of pages turning in an old copy of *Jacob's Room*.

The sound of the CBC.

The sound of rain in February.

The sound of wind picking through dried fescues and sweetgrass in a chinook-cleared grassland.

The sound of suffering.

The sound of chickadees in chinook weather.

The sound of jet engines.

The sound of public transit.

The sound of solidarity blockades on rail lines.

The sound of crowds in the Puerta del Sol, Madrid.

The sound of Twitter.

The sound of shoes.

The sound of a lizard scuttling across the warm bricks on the pathway in the garden at noon.

The sound of cars, cars, cars.

The sound of budget cuts.

The sound of parrots.

The sound of leap day.

The sound of quarantines.

The sound of stock market rallies and crashes.

The sound of the different regional accents of Spain.

The sound of wine being poured.

The sound of horns honking and feet moving.

The sound of voices through thin walls.

The sound of the state of exception.

The sound of birds in the warm Madrid morning as the lockdown begins.

The sound of anxious travellers.

The sound of airplanes.

The sound of relief upon landing in Calgary.

The sound of minus twenty weather.

The sound of snowplows.

The sound of the people of Italy, singing from their balconies.

I

Green in nature is one thing, green in literature another. Nature
and letters seem to have a natural antipathy; bring them together
and they tear each other to pieces.
– Virginia Woolf, *Orlando*

I have come to the conclusion that much can be learned about music by devoting oneself to the mushroom.
– John Cage, *Silence*

What is it about the touch of wood grain, that it can suddenly call to
mind the sensuous music of several lifetimes? It is a Friday and I am
thinking about tables. I am thinking about the ideal table, about the
Platonic form of the table, as I sit at one of the two farmhouse tables
that have come into our household. One is used for dinner – as well
as for writing, for games, for hospitality, for tea – while the other is
upstairs, pressed into service to house writing projects and stacks of
books and papers. The one in the dining room occupies my thoughts
today. I touch the dark grain of the wood. Every line in the table is

another year of carbon sequestration, another spring, a summer, a fall, a winter. The table is made of oak, though I am not the most reliable at discerning these things. My maternal grandfather bought it for five dollars at a farm auction more than fifty years ago. I think of it as one of those auctions that took place when a farm went belly up or the family opted to vamoose – or when someone passed away with debts that needed to be cleared. I don't know which kind, precisely, this table came from. There are dates written in pencil on its bottom. The first date is 1923, when the table was made. The original table was round, built to expand with the insertion of leaves. It is a pedestal table, with four supports jutting out from a central, square column. Throughout my childhood, the table was unfinished and regularly needed to be oiled. It squeaked when I applied my elbows to its surface, the top groaning as I leaned on it. It is now onto its third generation in my family – fourth, if one counts my children, who may one day choose to keep it in turn. It has been a focal point for revelry, welcome and gathering – the music that makes up our lives – for nearly a century.

〉

This book is about listening and land. It follows my belief that listening, or a lack thereof, has become a social and environmental problem. In this book, I argue that listening to landscapes, and doing so with dedication over a long period of time, is one path through this thicket. Listening has a role to play at this moment in our world. I start from my dining-room table and move out into the world from there. It has been an ongoing process, one that is open-ended and, necessarily for me, unfinished – as we always are, as long as we still have breath with which to speak.

〉

We were at the cinema in the beforetime, watching the latest installment of the *Star Wars* franchise. I can't recall which film now. *Episode VIII*? *Rogue One*? *Solo*? The franchise makes money and the films proliferate. These new films try to recapture a magic that, for me, was pretty well spent by 1983, when *Return of the Jedi* was released, yet still they continue. Anyhow, we were watching one of the new films, in the darkened cinema. The film ended. The iconic John Williams closing music began. The credits started to roll on that familiar field of stars in deepest space. One of my children leaned over to me and said, with the certainty of youth, "There aren't that many stars!"

≀

What world will we leave behind for our children and for those of our friends and family? Will there be a world that will be inhabitable? Signs at recent protests remind us that there is no Planet B. I was born into the very end of Generation X, but I couldn't quite identify with Douglas Coupland's particular brand of ennui. It was just a little bit too old for me somehow. Nor am I part of the so-called Generation Y, nor a millennial either. I grew up in the 1980s and 1990s, years of major geopolitical change. Reaganomics and Thatcherism. The fall of the Berlin Wall. The Montréal Massacre. The so-called end of alternatives to capitalism. Globalization. Mine is the first generation, we are told, that might have less than our parents did. In the US, especially in this era of the pandemic, life expectancies seem to be tipping toward a decline. But I was also born into the public uptake of environmentalism, launched by the generation that read Rachel Carson's *Silent Spring*. In the 1980s our heroes were people like David Suzuki, who showed us a world in peril on TV. Suzuki said that one of his errors was not planning for a long-term environmental movement, believing that they needed to succeed right away in changing the future. I met Suzuki when I was about six years old at an event at the University of British Columbia. It was an event about marine life. I remember him showing me a horseshoe crab. If I am honest, though, mostly I remember the crab. It scuttled with a seeming prehistoric calm across the sandy bed of the water table. It was a time when we watched and listened as, one by one, species disappeared and the stars were extinguished.

§

All of these things flashed through my mind when my child remarked that George Lucas and Co. must have been exaggerating the number of stars that exist in the night sky. My children, I realized, had never seen the night. They had never seen or heard the night in its spread-out glory. Living in cities drenched in evermore artificial light, drowning in seas of traffic noise, the stars continue to vanish and to be silenced as they age. We happen to live in one of the world's most light-polluted cities. While we were busy retying our bootlaces, or making tomorrow's lunch, or reading the business section, bit by bit we had been a small part of extinguishing the night. With the loss of the stars, I feel, too, the extinguishing of the ability to dream of a better, different world than the one in which we now live.

§

When I was a child, there were stars. I camped out under the stars, watching the glowing eyes of coyotes flicker in the starlight at the edge of the forest. I travelled to visit my grandparents in northern Alberta often. We would go in the summer and at Christmastime. Easter and Thanksgiving when possible. On winter visits, we would cut down Christmas trees – spruce, pine – from the farm's bushlands. We would eat turkeys raised by the neighbours and beef raised by my family from cows that had had jaunty names like T-Bone. And there were stars. The early setting sun vanished to reveal a pouring stream of white light extending across the night's sky, constellations sometimes lost amidst the brilliant glow of the stars under a new moon. The northern lights flashed green across the skies on some nights, purpling at the edges. The loud rush of space, the grinding of celestial music just past the bounds of hearing.

≀

But there are no family farms to return to any longer. There haven't been those cold, crisp, brilliant nights in my children's lives. The occasional satellite crossing the sky is no longer a rarity and a treat. Now the sky is full of glittering junk.

≀

I thought that we had done a good job of connecting our children to the land, but it was clear that we had work to do. So we made it a project to find the stars. As a family, we ventured farther back-country, looping into the mountains near Jasper. We were devoured by mosquitoes while the trees listened to our footsteps. It rained and was cloudy on that trip. While we reached new levels of off-grid prowess, there were no stars. We made other attempts in Banff, Lake Louise and across the prairies and parklands of Alberta. At length we were successful, sleeping outside of the tent on one beautiful, clear night near Revelstoke, British Columbia. After the moon went down, we woke, dew-covered, in the very early morning, to see a panoply of stars scattered across the darkness. It was not a bright winter's night, but it would have to do. We dried our sleeping bags in the morning sun and spoke about what lies out there in the night.

≀

The night bears listening to. It bears witnessing. Like so much of the environment – like the forests, the rivers and watersheds, the grasslands – the night is being obliterated through a series of human actions. It is for this set of reasons, then, that I have come to write about environments in a new way. I am learning about birds and trees through a new lens. Not simply to understand a world that we are in the midst of losing, but also to learn what I might do to forestall the collapse.

ξ

As I worked at my table, I watched the seasons turn, the weather turn. I looked out the window at clear skies, at rain, at snow and at a new type of weather that I don't remember from my childhood – smoke. There were no stars on smoky nights. A thick pall scratched at our throats, reddening our eyes. With that burn, we passed more nights without the sky's imagination, with losses untold and incalculable.

ξ

This project began, then, as a response to questions that my children asked, either directly or indirectly, about how to live in this world. My children made me ask myself the same questions. This book is an insufficient answer, but it's a start. And then, during the pandemic, I spoke – over the phone, over the computer – and exchanged messages – over the computer, over paper – with people in many places. We shared our feelings of befuddlement, confusion, stress and disarray. We wondered how the world had become so fast, and we wondered about what happened when it all stopped. The slow movement that had already emerged in response to the culture of speed provided one avenue for engagement, but access to a culture of slow is uneven in a world that has become more and more characterized by precarious forms of work. The economy has become one in which your speed is often tied to your earnings and determines your ability to thrive, or to survive. Until we hit a collective pause and heard it fall apart.

≀

The response that I've arrived at, my turn to listening to the land, might not be for everyone. It requires a commitment to attention and attentiveness, a commitment to developing a capacity for compassion and care. This listening calls us to take care of others and of the land on which we stand. It demands time, and time is in short supply for many people, for many reasons.

≀

Learning to listen is a profound, political act. Listening, when done with deliberate measure, is an act of defiance. What remains unheard remains unacknowledged. I have now spent the last several years learning to listen as though everyone and everything around me matters in the utmost. I've started with the night's sky and moved from there. Listening has provided me with a way to come back to the world with fresh ears. I learned in the process that I was very tired. I still am, but at least now I have a small spark that comes from listening. This listening provides me with a new way to return to the environment from which my family comes. This change has proven to be important during the global pandemic. All of a sudden, the world became much, much quieter. Human sounds slackened, slowed and in some cases even ceased for a short while. Listening took on renewed power. It led me back to having some kind of hope.

≀

Think of the 1980s in North American cities. When I was young, I lived first in Ontario, then in Vancouver and then spent much of my childhood in Calgary. In Vancouver, our townhouse was brown on the outside and brown on the inside. In the back, cedar hedges tasted of sap when we darted in and out of them, playing tag or hide-and-seek. It was a time of shag carpets and wood panelling, leftovers from the 1970s. Our wood-burning fireplace was made of rough brick. One day a burning brand leapt from it, rolling aflame across the carpet. I thought my father very brave for picking up the log and returning it to the fire. No big deal. But I held onto that detail. A small burn mark was left on the carpet, spoiling the pile, the soft swish-swish of feet in socks. What remains is always so unpredictable, so wavy, so variable.

≀

My first memory of listening to music is from that time, in that same room. My mother set the needle on the record player. The Beatles, *1962–1966*, a best-of compilation of their early music. Ringo Starr's easy one-two beats; John Lennon and Paul McCartney's harmonics, guitar and bass; and George Harrison, playing with restraint and poise. I still don't have a favourite Beatle. Each had a strength. I would age and then turn to their later music, the psychedelic era of Sgt. Pepper proving to me to be the most compelling. But we started with the early melodies: "She Loves You," "I Want to Hold Your Hand," "Eight Days a Week." Mom endeavoured to teach me to recognize the rhythm of the songs, clapping to the beat along with Ringo's drum kit. I tried. I got it wrong. Mom showed me again. I tried again. I failed anew. Was it one day or many days? At length, I started to get the idea. But I was a slow study. It was like my inability to jump until very late – so late that my parents grew concerned. Listening sometimes takes a while.

≀

When I was a younger version of me, I also had a lot of ear infections. They gave me antibiotics for the aches. I lived many of my early years with ringing in my ears and the taste of banana-flavoured medicine in my mouth. After some time, the doctors did a surgery to puncture and put tubes in each of my eardrums. I was scared on the way into the operating theatre, but I was told that it was for the best. That way the fluids that built up behind my eardrums would be able to drain. Later, I remember lying on a hot compress, one side and then the other, waiting for my ears to drain. And then the back-of-the-throat release when the fluid let go.

⸘

The problem with listening is that hearing is not evenly distributed. Also, hearing is both a physiological response to stimulus and one of the most common metaphors in the English language. I hear you, friend! The tubes in my ears came out some years later. My healing eardrums pushed them most of the way out and they were removed in a doctor's office. The inflammations receded as I aged. Now my ears don't trouble me much. I did have one incapacitating round of tinnitus, and there is always a bit of background buzz, but that's all for now. The men in my family, however, seem to lose their hearing as they age. I anticipate the same.

⸘

I was told that I would have some hearing loss in my right ear from all of the childhood brouhaha. Not many people know this about me. Also, I was born with a superfluous third earlobe just in front of my left ear. No, really. Another doctor burned it off in his office. I miss that extra flap of skin. What would Freud say about that? A hearing test a few years ago couldn't find any hearing loss. I do struggle, though, to hear in spaces with ambient sound. Like when I saw an old friend a while ago, one whom I hadn't seen in a couple of years. It was an evening before the pandemic. We were walking down the streets of Dublin. Our feet sounded on the flag- and cobblestones. The noise of revelry spilled from the bars as we passed. We had both been enjoying some Irish beers and whiskeys. My friend was struggling with the low-level illnesses that come with parenthood. He was unable to hear from one of his ears, a result of a two-year-long infection. He didn't know, yet, if the damage would be permanent. I switched sides with him so that we could converse. We had both had experiences with hearing challenges, but my situation had recovered. Sometimes the solutions aren't as simple as just switching sides. Every time I hear or read a listening metaphor – listen up! Hear hear! – I think of who is invited into this listening and who is left out. You know what I'm saying?

⁊

The school that I attended from the seventh grade onward was home to special programs. It included programs for students with giftedness, programs for students with learning disabilities and programs then known as being for the deaf and hard of hearing. From a young age, I became used to seeing sign language interpreters at gatherings. Students in our school tended to learn – taught themselves when necessary – American Sign Language, whether or not they could hear, so that they could communicate across the classroom, soundlessly.

⁊

Throughout those years in school, I headed north often. My mother's parents had worked a farm north of the Athabasca River in northern Alberta in an area known as Richmond Park. Half of that side of my family was Polish. The records that I have tell me that they came to Canada from Silesia, a region in Poland and what is now the northern end of the Czech Republic. The other half of the maternal side of my family is a mix of Irish and French. That family farm, now sold, lies in Treaty 8 territory. On the other side of my family, my father's parents worked a farm south of the Athabasca River in an area known as Meanook. One half of that side was English. The town of Kendal, England, seems to have been some sort of origin point. The other half of the family was Highland Scots and from parts of Eastern Europe. Their farm, also now sold, lies in Treaty 6 territory. As I grew up, I learned more from listening to my grandparents' stories, their lands, and the absences and gaps in the tales than I have from perhaps anything else.

⁂

My paternal grandmother, Granny, was known in the community as Kay, short for Kathleen. She was born into modest circumstances in Edmonton and, after meeting my grandfather – Ken – at university, moved north as they started up their farming life together. She was educated, thoughtful, political and caring. I relished my time with her. Granny's job as a teacher in the nearest town's elementary school, late in her life and after her kids had grown, brought her into a wide range of contacts with the world. One time, she hosted children's entertainer and singer Fred Penner in the community. I watched Penner on CBC as a child. His cassettes were frequent companions on our road trips. I think of him every time that I make a sandwich. Granny got me one of Penner's records and got him to autograph it in both of our names. During the pandemic, after twenty-five years or so, I found the record in an old box that I brought over from my parents' house. The box – and the albums – were dusty, but the dedication was fresh. There, linked through music, were Granny's and my names.

⁂

A few years ago, in the beforetime, I was travelling to give a talk. In transit, I happened to be in the departures lounge of the Ottawa airport. I ended up standing in line for a smoothie behind Fred Penner. At first, I didn't think that I would say anything, shy as I usually am. Then a woman about my age came up and asked him if he was indeed Fred Penner. He confirmed that he was. She said something kind and then carried on. He and I then fell into conversation. I ended up telling him about my granny, and about his own visit to northern Alberta all those years ago. He said that he recalled his visit and Granny as well. We happened to order the same smoothie, then went on our ways.

⁊

The times change. A couple of winters ago, there was a mountain of snow in our small backyard. The flower bed, crowned by a crabapple tree, alongside a honeysuckle and miniature lilac shrub, were all buried. I shovelled the snow off the bricked-in patio and the drainage canal, with its collection of river rocks that I have quietly been adding to. The snow that year piled high, right to the edge of the six-foot fence when the snow was at its deepest. The dog – that was the year he was a puppy – clambered to the top, nibbling at the higher branches of the dormant tree and peering into the neighbours' yard to see if their chihuahuas were about. I imagined our dog falling or leaping to the other side. It never happened.

⁊

The next winter, there was no snow to speak of in mid-March. There was crust and ice, but the ground was by and large clear. Our morning walks detoured around the icy paths that lay in the perpetual shade of the north sides of buildings. But snow was scarce. Determined to ski one weekend, we drove an hour and a half down the

Spray Lakes Road to Mount Shark, high in the Kananaskis Range. There the snows were beautiful, crisp, fantastic. But what would usually be a wintry drive home was a brown, calm one undertaken in warm weather. Yes, there is significant variation year to year under the eastern shadow of the Rocky Mountains. The chinook winds blow through in mid-winter, warming and melting the land. But the previous year had been the warmest on record in the world's oceans, the fourth warmest at the time in terrestrial temperatures, and science concurs – in an overwhelming balance – that calamitous change is afoot.

≀

Winter is part of my annual cycle too. It is a quiet time of labour – often the hardest-working months of the year – and part of the renewal that each cycle around the sun brings to us. Without the cold of winter, I feel bereft. I mourn for the climate in a way that is difficult to pin down. Perhaps what people call ecological grief. Or perhaps the opposite of a seasonal affective disorder: an unseasonal affective disorder. Or unseasonal affective condition, because it doesn't seem like a disorder at all. What seems disordered is the temperature of the air outside. In the forest, I hear birds singing, whisky jacks active in the winter slowdown, and squirrels and chipmunks rousing – even if only for a short while – to head outdoors and see the conditions outside of their burrows.

≀

During the winters for the last few years, my radio listening has in part become an exercise of enduring the inanity of weather reports. "Great weather today," the CBC states again and again when the mercury indicates ten degrees above seasonal averages. "Looks like we're in for some bad weather," the hosts intone when skies darken with clouds that hold the snows that the land needs. On the one hand, I get it: these are not comments to be taken seriously. They are radio banter and would be just as inane on the other stations. As a pattern, though, this banter teaches listeners to spurn the winter and the graces that it offers to us.

⟨

The CBC is now tuned to Radio 2 and Brahms pours forth. Music is where much of the literature about listening spends its energy. With good reason. What do we listen to when we listen to music? If I play a song on my guitar, what do you hear? My mother worked hard to get me to clap along to the rhythm. I want to clap my hands and show her that I learned to have a sense of rhythm after all. Years later, I passed my grade three piano examination from the Royal Conservatory and then picked up a trumpet in band class. I built up to being lead trumpet by late in high school. Later still, I picked up a guitar and learned to strum some chords and play the Beatles' "Blackbird" and "Yellow Submarine," among other songs. I am not particularly skilled, but I was able to play "Baby Beluga" to my children when they were young. I have enough musical training to be able to tell Beethoven from Mozart most of the time, and always enough to tell the difference between the Beatles and the Rolling Stones. What does it mean to push the limits of listening, to be able to engage with the melodies that reach our ears? There is a certain training that comes from the listening that I have done, a certain training to hear the rhythms of a dominant culture. Only belatedly, and with a conscious care gained over time, have I come to the music that characterizes the lands on which I live. My training emphasized one kind of listening; I want another. What would that listening look like?

⟨

The twentieth-century composer John Cage provides me with some ways to start to think through my questions. The ruptures that he created with his music and performances feel on track, like he got much further down this path than I have yet. Cage is well known for his prompts toward listening and for his creation of the prepared piano, a modified instrument ready for unusual performances. I am listening to Cage's work right now as I write. As the silence of $4'33''$ – a famous three-movement piece composed entirely of silence – ensues and then endures, ambient noise becomes evermore pronounced. I strain to assemble the harmonies and melodies that unfold from everyday life. The piece was first performed in an outdoor setting, a detail that I find striking for considering how the piece works. Cage was inspired, the story goes, by his encounter with an anechoic chamber. An anechoic chamber is a room designed to absorb all sound. That is, it is a room designed not to have any echo. Those who experience such a space report finding it very disorienting. After all, most humans operate in part by constantly calibrating in relation to the sounds in which we are immersed. Cage went into the room in order to experience a perfectly silent space. What he found, however, was not silence, but its opposite. Upon leaving the room, he reported hearing two things: a low sound and a high sound. The first of those things, Cage was told, was his circulatory system. It was the sound of the blood pumping through his veins and of the steady work of his heart. The second sound was said to be the hum of his nervous system, a whine that operates at a pitch and frequency that humans normally can't register. Accounts vary, though, and one might say that it was just ringing in his ears, the everyday sounds of tinnitus. Either way, Cage became convinced that there was no such thing as silence. Sound is continuous in our lives. Sound is even generated by the operations of our own bodies.

⸙

Like Cage, the Canadian composer R. Murray Schafer notes that our bodies have sonic properties. Through research that he conducted as part of the World Soundscape Project, he learned about how the world adjusts and tunes people as listeners. His team observed that countries' different electronic signatures impact us in unexpected ways. The different alternating and direct currents of electrical grids create different sounds, and there is a slight hum in the background. It is always there when you are indoors or in the city, power lines buzzing overhead or underfoot while you nap in the hammock, while you do your sun salutations or while you brew your espresso. Schafer's observation was that the natural pitch chanted by meditators seemed to vary according to geographical location. Even more than that, he suggested that the natural pitch of these practitioners tended to align with the pitch of the electrical currents in their environments. The tale might be a bit apocryphal, but the idea is enthralling. As we struggle to listen to others as well as to ourselves, we must make some very fine adjustments to our own bodies in order to account for our sonic geographies.

꙳

As I age, I find myself listening to different music. I find it a struggle to identify with most contemporary music. Much of it, I realize, is marketed for a different demographic – my children's. This disjunction helps me to realize that the music I listened to in my youth was a product of markets as much as it was any sort of youthful rebellion, even if I still want to be optimistic about Kurt Cobain's tragic life. Markets contain us and anticipate us. It's quite possible that you realized this set of facts sooner than I did – I feel belated, late to the show. More and more, an orchestra works better for me than a drum kit, two guitars and a bass. The most moving performance that I have seen this past decade was the Calgary Philharmonic Orchestra in concert with Wolastoqiyik tenor Jeremy Dutcher. Dutcher's sustained voice, ringing out across the performance hall above the piano and strings was enchanting, transfixing. That evening's orchestral performance was astonishing. Behind that performance must come the ballet to commemorate the life and music of Leonard Cohen, whose gravel-jewelled voice makes evermore sense to me. I listen to wordless music while I am writing in order to distinguish my thoughts from the world. Voice is mostly gone from this workday repertoire, unless I am frustrated. On those days I often turn to Mozart's Requiem. I understand Glenn Gould more and more. I can now appreciate the 1981 recording of the Goldberg Variations, humming and all, whereas earlier I could only enjoy the 1955 performance of the eccentric, exuberant youngster. Times change, my ears change. The seasons change.

}

Music is not only made up of the deliberate compositions replayed by musicians. I think of the quiet stillness of listening to what, in Albertan terms, is the north. Listening to the north is a private event, even when we share it with one another. Think of winter, of the crisp silence of snow that noises underfoot as you walk. The silence of an overhead night sky that hits your ears as wind crosses the fields. The nighttime crackle becomes an aurora of rippling sound. How do we describe the sound that nothing makes? Bumpy rides in old pickups, half-tons with creaky springs in their bench seats and suspensions, cranky transmissions. The smell of stale cigarette smoke has its own sound somehow – the long-after residues of tobacco and paper, burning through a filter, the rough inhalations of my late grandfather. An old AM radio, static. Listening to the north is something that lingers. I listen to ideas, to sounds, to my own breath. The north has other ideas for me.

}

Outdoors, cattle call to one another. Their lowing sound is different on a winter's morning – it is less urgent, but somehow keener. It is as though the cold is a prompt for bovine reflection on the passage of time. Sheep call too, bleating and jangling; a small flock pushing out of the crooked barn. Dogs bark. In the trees, the usual bird calls are silent. The trees creak and moan, nurse their sore joints in the chill. In a few places, the leaves have dried and stayed on the branches. Those dry leaves rustle, rustle, stay. One breaks off and falls to the ground, but its landing is muffled by the snows. In the evening, as the skies clear, the coyotes howl and yip en masse, sounding as though they are just outside the window. Sometimes they are very close – you can hear them crossing the yard – or was it one of the dogs? The coyotes become bold when the dogs forget to bark back. So the dogs do bark back. The air is filled for a half-hour with a canine chorus of disagreement and disparagement. This sound too, you see, is music. Inside, the fire burns. The fuel releases heat and light and sound. The fire hisses, crackles, slips. The music of a gentle, burning warmth.

{

I sit at my table, pen in hand, scratching on the page. A recording of Tomaso Albinoni's works is playing now. Outside it is the first day of serious snowfall. The snow will melt, although I wish that it would stay. The roads are terrible and people are struggling to get up the hills in their cars – let alone to walk through the now knee-high drifts – yet I love the snow. It has so many qualities. I look out the window: The snow is clinging to the spruces. It is perched on the half-bare deciduous trees in our small inner-city square. Pillars and fence posts are gathering jaunty caps of white, a foot high and deepening. The houses are piling up puffs and drifts in the eaves, at the points where one angle of roof meets another. The snow continues to fall. Snowfall is sensual weather. Snow is inviting, enveloping. It is not cold to the touch. Rather, it melts as it contacts your skin, a layer of wet forming where the body's warmth thaws it. Deep snow provides heavy insulation. When it lies thick on the ground it is time to gather inside, to get warm under the covers. It is perhaps not a coincidence that July, August and September are the most common months for birthdays in Canada.

⁊

Snow has tremendous sonic properties. People who live in northern climates know this fact well. Snow muffles sound. It gives city-dwellers respite from the daily hubbub. In the forest after a fresh snowfall the air is crisp, deep and silent. Snow falling from a nearby branch cuts through the air, but most distant sounds fall away. Underfoot, the snow crunches and squeaks – different pitches, intensities and sounds for different degrees of cold – and it whooshes down from higher up. On mountains, snow makes a distinct *whumpf* sound when, after building up in weight, it falls down upon itself. That sound comes when heavy new snow fractures the crystalline facet layers that have built up underneath. *Whumpfing* snows are portents of avalanches to come: the sound tells you that the snow is breaking free of the bonds that have held it in place. The sound lets you know that the rush of a snowslide is likely to follow. Always look uphill in winter. Keep your ears open. Cross open spaces with tact and efficiency, putting room between you and your loved ones. Know the spruces and the pines. Listen to their advice on a snow-covered mountainside. Watch out, though, for tree wells. These areas, right around the taller trees, are where conifers' skirts of needles leave hollows of shallow snow. They can be traps in which intrepid travellers can become locked in a wintry embrace.

⁊

Snowfall perks up our ears as the noise falls away. It is an invitation to pay attention to what stands before us – an invitation to presence in the moment and into the indoors, too: the warmth of a winter's fire, a warm blanket, a mug of coffee.

ξ

To listen to the sensuality of the outdoors has become a struggle in this time. My everyday life, for instance, has at least two types of time in it, one in competition with the other. One muffles listening, the other sharpens it. I think that this may be true for you too, which is why I share it. Most days, the push and pull sounds like two different musical scores being played at the same time, with the volume going up and down on each. For the sake of brevity, let's call the first of these scores industrial time and the second one listening time.

ξ

For the first, think of electronic schedules and time management systems. So many people carry theirs on their phones. The system enables many great things: speedy communication, fast collaboration, efficient planning. On some days I rush from one meeting to the next, striving to maintain good work in a timely manner. There is consistently more to do than can ever be managed. We have long since known the signs in each other: tired eyes; quick, noncommittal greetings and a push to get down to business. We turn to our agendas. Beeping devices indicate the next event. This relentless consumption of time works against the call of the migrating geese or the swish of trees pushing up outside of the new library and its fresh landscaping. We turn our collars against the incipient cold and move along, ignoring the music of the seasons.

ξ

The second sort of time, listening time, is more interesting to me. I am reminded every day of its possibility by my granny, even though she died many years ago. I received her day planner after her passing; it is a little leather-bound ring binder into which I faithfully insert new calendar sheets each year. I use this planner every day. It's beside me now, more than two decades later. I have come by many other pieces of Granny's life over time, but her day planner ended up being my most direct inheritance. It's small and brown. A stamp inside tells me that it was made in Canada. It accepts six-hole refill pages, which they still make. The space for individual days is sometimes too small. Many of my days are a mess of scribbled notes. Because I carry it with me regularly, the brown leather has darkened over time. Oils from my skin saturate the exterior unevenly, as have tea spills and the stains of many lunches. You might argue that day planners aren't much – or any – less industrial than phone-based planners. You wouldn't really be wrong. This planner was bought in a store. While it is of high quality, it likely wasn't a source of great sentiment for Granny. But it is for me. Every time that I open it, the pages flapping apart, the splitting leather creaking a mild protest, I think of her. She taught me which plants were edible and showed me how to feed chickens. Granny showed me, indirectly perhaps, what time might mean from the perspective of a birch tree's sigh. We do not, in the end, get to control what our legacies will be, and these are hers for me. I suppose that we each do the best that we can and hope for kindness. And so, in that creaking spine of my day planner, I am reminded, every time, that there is a sort of temporality beyond the everyday. This time can be circular, not linear. It is linked to a broader web of life of which I am a small part. The time of my living is something that I cup in the palm of my hands, listening.

❧

It is finally cold. The years 2014, 2015, 2016, 2017, 2018, 2019, 2020 and 2021 are officially the warmest ever recorded so far. I fear that it may be too late for us. Yes, even with the pandemic having led to a one-time drop in greenhouse gas emissions. I was worried that the cold wouldn't come and I am glad that it is here at last. Climate change, "they" say, has a public relations problem. Perhaps it has several. For the most part, climate change is too slow-moving and abstract for people to get their minds around. I know that I struggle on this point. The climate deals in a different kind of time than industrial time. It becomes easy to conflate the weather with the climate. Our brains, unable to think at the scales needed to understand how our everyday actions impact our children's and grandchildren's futures – perhaps trained to think in this way by the everyday world – simply give up trying. Or, to think about it differently, the horror of what may come is too great. Instead of listening to the doom being prophesied, many of us turn our environmental watchdogs into so many Cassandras as we stop up our ears. Listening isn't easy. I think of this work of listening as part of what Trevor Herriot calls "the work of atonement that stands before all prairie people today." Atonement for what? Lost opportunities, Herriot suggests. He writes about how the prairie grasslands have been destroyed over time by agriculture and private land use systems. He laments the loss of Indigenous ways of managing the land that predated colonization, as well as the loss of the Métis land use systems that were disrupted in the wake of the Northwest Resistance and the execution of Louis Riel. With those losses came shrinking prairies, loss of habitat and exploitation of the land. All settlers on the Prairies are implicated in this history, which is by no means in the past. So how to atone? Herriot is accompanied on the prairies by the Métis teacher Norman Fleury. Fleury is a dedicated instructor of Michif, the language of the Métis. Fleury notes that the past was hard, but that it involved co-operation. "It was sometimes only by helping each other," Fleury says, "that we got through terrible and difficult times." How do we come together? (Especially when the pandemic has forced us to be apart?) You may have wondered about this question. I know that some days it is easier to get behind the wheel, turn on the heated seats and imagine ourselves to be separate from the past. But it is only easy in the short term, and it is only easy for some, for those who have the means to do so. In the longer term, the land is suffering, the elk herds are in rapid decline in the north, the butterflies are being killed during their delicate migrations to the south and if the bee populations collapse because of illness, or pesticides, or exhausts, or invasive species – let alone imported species of hornets – then humans will be scrambling to pollenate flowers by hand. They are already doing so in some places. It's best, in other words, to atone while we can. Let it not be a planetary deathbed confession.

⁊

While we are atoning, how shall we think about oil, here in Alberta? In a book concerned with this place, the question is inevitable. You may already have been asking when I would get around to the subject. How could I not speak about oil? Don't worry, I will. Maybe not as much as you would like. Maybe too much. Maybe not as easily as some might like. But I will and I do. The region where my family settled lies at the edge of the boreal forest, farmlands cut back from the trees, with muskegs and sloughs draining through the farms. It is a land that can be both beautiful and brutal. I read tales of the beauty and the brutality online, posted by friends and relatives who live up there. I have witnessed both. And it still is both of those things even if I am not there to listen to it right now. The river – the Athabasca River – is perhaps best known to people in the south because of its association with Fort McMurray and its bitumen extraction projects. These have been at the heart of Alberta's – if not Canada's – war between the environment and the economy, though many may claim – in my view rightly – that that is a false opposition. I know the river a bit differently. Athabasca, the town, was once known as Athabasca Landing. It was a landing point, way back when, for boats and barges. It was a river port of trade, a place settled by Europeans for its furs. Then came the farms. Early in the twentieth century it was a rapidly growing hub. That was before the main rail line bypassed the place and before a fire in 1913 burned much of the new, speculation-driven town to the ground. The Athabasca River eventually flows into the Mackenzie Delta in the Northwest Territories via the Slave and Mackenzie Rivers. Its headwaters are upstream from the town of Jasper. From Jasper the river flows northeast, then dips south for a bit, where it runs through the town. Then the river turns and heads back north, through Fort McMurray and Fort McKay, before passing through Alberta's major bitumen reserves and then emptying into Lake Athabasca. The town that I know well is upstream from the pollution and the boom-and-bust prosperity associated with Fort Mac. But does oil not affect what it is that I want to say nonetheless? Or course it does. Many people among my family and friends have worked in oil. It may be a diminishing part of the economy now that the price of oil has crashed, yet again. (Of course, the province and business interests will surely fight for oil's recovery, even as oil itself may be moving into the past.) But it has been a major part of life in this province. My own wages far to the south have been paid in part from the royalties that come from oil. We will see what the future brings. The world and this place are changing, as Alberta writers like Kevin Van Tighem are noting. But oil marks all tales from Alberta in one way or another.

⸘

The epigraph to this book is the sonnet "Butterfly Bones: Sonnet Against Sonnets" by Margaret Avison. It is a wonderful sonnet – you can go back and look at it again if you would like – a tightly constructed fourteen-line poem in which the image of a butterfly, killed and mounted, is compared at length to the rigid form of the sonnet itself. The butterfly is a conceit, or an extended metaphor. Readers can see how language traps us all: we are inside a rigid set of codes that render life fragile and brittle. Languages, as well as the sonnet form, are both under scrutiny by Avison in the poem. "Fierce listening," the term that captures me when I read it, is something that the butterfly does – it exists, pinned to the board, in a mounted posture of "fierce listening." But does it listen at all, dead and pinned? Avison suggests that humans interfere with non-humans – in this case butterflies – when she holds open the possibility that the butterfly listens, though dead. Or is it us, trapped in the amber of language, who are listening for a way out? Avison's poem is ambiguous on this point. Do we, can we, listen? I want to extend the image. I see the butterfly in a Zen stance, in a position of meditative listening or perhaps in a position of contemplation. The contemplative position is more akin to Avison's Christianity. I don't share Avison's religious commitments, but I can respect them in this context. What does it mean to contemplate? Can we listen and remain open after the formaldehyde and the pin? Can we listen prior to pain? Or is it the pain of being affixed into language – let alone the pain of the world – that opens us up to a butterfly's ears? Whatever answers one might come up with, the butterfly's posture of fierce listening strikes me as the right one. It is an ethical choice, a silence that is anything but passive.

≀

I am here in order to listen, but what does it mean to listen? More often than not, listening serves as a metaphor, just as the concept of reading does. When I "listen," I am often doing so by reading, or by seeing, or by bearing witness to the world around me. Although much of the writing on listening is about music and how music works, listening extends outward. Listening is about hearing, but it is also about sight, perhaps also taste, touch and smell – and then back all over again. I cannot imagine listening to the peaty musk of mushrooms growing on the forest floor without my sense of smell. What is the significance of listening's metaphorical reach? If I am here, writing at my dining-room table, in order to listen and to bear witness, then listening becomes a political act. It is a sense needed in order to make peace in an often loud world. Listening may be one of the key political crises of our time. In an age when the push is, over and over again, to enunciate – and to do so loudly – how can we listen? Audre Lorde's famous line "your silence will not protect you" is a truth that I have sought to take to heart. Yet listening is needed in order to complete the act of speaking. It allows us to feel for one another. Without listening, there is no speech. Without silence to receive words, there is only noise. Lorde's speaker also needs listeners. We need to listen and to view that listening as a politically meaningful mode of engagement. Listening to birdsong is a choice that is bounded by time and by location and by a decision to pay attention to that one certain thing, though it is also determined by the privilege of being able to do so. It follows that listening to birdsong also requires a commitment to the environment, because without it there are no flycatchers, warblers or larks for us to hear in their exaltations. Listening, when done with deliberation and care, is loud.

꙰

I think of St. Augustine of Hippo as an important example of the impacts of listening. His *Confessions*, written around AD 400, provides the first written record of silent reading. Augustine left northern Africa in order to visit the already famous St. Ambrose in Milan. When he saw him, he was shocked to discover Ambrose reading – silently. Ambrose, he wrote, might have moved his lips as he read, but no sound came out. This fact was amazing to Augustine. In his day, hand-copied manuscripts were taken to be prompts for the spoken word, or even as crutches for the memory of that word. It was a time when, in the West, memory and oral culture were just beginning to be overtaken by a culture of reading and writing. I think of the quiet intimacies that we share with books. I find those moments remarkable. Or I think of the intimacies that we share by passing books that we have read and loved between one another. The silence of our reading is part of the charge of sharing. But think of chants and songs reverberating in ancient cathedrals, too. These have their own intimacy. Ambrose's silent act was a radical one, and it was an act with far-reaching consequences as literacy spread. Silent reading would become more and more common as the codex style of book-making came into fashion – what you and I think of as a book, rather than a scroll – and, later, when the mass production of books via the printing press made them so much less expensive.

ɣ

Writers of book history must also take note of another key passage in the *Confessions*: Augustine's moment of enlightenment in the garden. Not unlike Isaac Newton under his apple tree or the Buddha with his Bodhi tree, Augustine, seated under a fig tree, experienced his own moment of revelation. It happens when, as he describes it, he heard the voice of a child in a nearby house. He then listened to the voice's request. "Tolle, lege," is what Augustine heard. "Take it and read." Taking the scriptures in hand, Augustine read. He chose a random passage that happened to be from the book of Romans. This passage inspired him for the rest of his life. His listening and then reading led to his abandoning his previous worldly entanglements. Reading the Bible put him on the long path to canonization – that is, to his becoming a saint. I am fond of this passage. It shows such a clear link between listening and hearing, as well as between listening to words and developing self-awareness from reading. There is no reason why Augustine couldn't just have told readers that he was inspired by the Bible. In fact, the spoken words that bring him to the Word are unnecessary to the story. It was a common practice to open the scriptures and pick a passage at random. But readers are told that there were spoken words that Augustine heard. We are also told that this act of listening lead to the written words that change his life. So these words – "Tolle, lege" – must not be accidental. They are there on purpose, as part of the events as Augustine recorded them. So they are important. How so? This passage seems to be about more than the link between spoken and written words. It is about the necessity of listening and understanding. Had Augustine not had that inspiration in the garden, then his worldly life – which he describes as being dissolute – would likely have continued. We wouldn't have a Catholic saint named Augustine. No enduring book would have accompanied his life. Instead, Augustine listened. Doing so resulted in him leading what he viewed as a good life.

≀

Augustine sold his possessions and donated property to the Church. He became a monk and then a bishop. Taking to heart the criticism that the Book offered to him meant a profound change. As for me, I am still learning how to listen and how to change. I am learning to understand the contradictions of my family's love and care for the land and environment and entanglement in petroleum cultures, for instance. I am learning to listen to the pain of aquifers that I am complicit in polluting, waterways that my actions contribute to disturbing and birds whose flight patterns my own terrestrial patterns disrupt. I am listening to the news reports of burning forests and rising temperatures, changing seasons. I am listening to news that the pandemic has lessened human impacts on the world, even if only for a brief moment. I am learning that my generation is already failing the generation that is now coming into the world. When I stepped outside, before the pandemic, I heard idling cars, leaf blowers, lawn mowers, traffic and the buzz of mobile phones pinging messages through the ether. I seldom heard children laughing and playing. I intermittently heard the wind, the trees rustling. Some days, it felt as though the world was trying to shrug her shoulders and cast off the mantle of human messiness. And now I do not know what to think. I hear an imperilled time, one with the song of cicadas, crickets, grasshoppers and the trill of birds, chickadees on the wing. Arctic terns. Those last birds, the terns, I learn from my birding book, may see the most sunlight of any species. They migrate from the South Pole to the North, travelling swiftly through Alberta. I hear my children's questions about why the world is the way that it is and I hope that, together, we can hear their desires for inheriting the future.

≹

There are so many things that I have inherited: My grandfather's belt buckle. The daily-use farm dishes – or at least the ones that haven't been broken. The family silver. Granny's day planner. A nagging feeling of doubt. The dining-room tables from both family farms. The family piano. A love of country music. The chairs for the dining-room tables from both family farms. The fear that a good year portends a worse year to come. The knowledge of which plants are good to eat. A love of gardening, baking and canning. A blue trunk with brass trim. Copies of Kierkegaard's *Philosophical Fragments, Fear and Trembling* and *The Sickness Unto Death*. A copy of Granny's master's thesis. The need to be outdoors. A persistent worry about brain tumours. A pair of old snowshoes. Three framed prints that used to hang in the farmhouse. Several pieces of Cree art from northern Alberta. About twenty farmer hats from farm supply and explosives companies. A love of open skies and wide horizons. A thirst to visit other places. My grandfather's Stetson.

≀

The conditions of the time during which I wrote this book keep breaking in, pushing in from the margins and becoming the centre of it all. My love of open skies and wide horizons took me, in early January of 2020, to the Banff Centre for Arts and Creativity, and then, between February and March, to central Spain. There I rented a small flat in the city of Salamanca, where I was a guest at the university. The apartment, just on the edge of the old city, was a quiet, well-appointed one. My partner and I were there together initially, before she went home. I hadn't brought a mobile phone and we only discovered upon arrival that the apartment was without an Internet connection. I spent my days walking across the old city, through the main square, enjoying coffees on terraces, giving lectures and writing. At night, I listened to the sound of the birds flapping up off the streets when cars passed. The tapas places all along the road were visited every night by the people of the city. In the mornings I ran through the park and along the Río Tormes. The ancient city and its medieval university, all surmounted by its cathedral, provided a calm respite. Spain provided me with the distance needed to be able to examine Alberta anew, from an ocean away. The words poured forth until the pandemic cut everything short.

≀

I had travelled to Spain before. On a previous trip, we went to the hills near Salamanca. It was an October day and so it was cooler overnight than it might have been. The daytime was still warm. It was sunny, crisp. Early in the day, we strolled through La Alberca, a village that had been settled by the French during what is still locally called the Reconquista. It was, our guide told us, a spiritual village. Every evening a woman in black walked the streets, tolling a bell to summon people's souls back to their homes. Doorways were surmounted by crosses, stones were carved with sigils of Mary and Jesus. We stopped in the dark stone church and looked at the Spanish iconography. There were many bleeding Jesuses; Christ's wounds were depicted in detail. The town pig – who every year wandered the streets until its appointed time came – was nowhere in sight, and cured ham was on sale in every shop. After the town, we visited a mountaintop monastery known as Peña de Francia, which is sometimes part of pilgrimage routes. The mountain, capped by a sundial, provided views in all directions while a pair of buzzards circled on the updrafts. We toured through empty monastic cells before heading back into the valley. We chatted amongst ourselves, our feet scudding on chipped flints. The wind cut through our light clothes and we put on more layers. We drove back down the mountaintop and ate lunch in a welcoming countryside restaurant. Large servings of meats and vegetables were accompanied by wine and followed with aperitifs, home-brewed shots of flavoured alcohol. After lunch, we walked the small village of Mogarraz. An artist had painted images based on photographs taken for identity cards during Francisco Franco's rule. The paintings of each of the three-hundred-plus former inhabitants had been matched to their homes and affixed to the exterior walls. The paintings were expressive, completed in a minimalist palette of greys and browns in keeping with the photographs on which they were based. The village has been enjoying a small bump in tourism as a result of these paintings.

౨

One of the locals with whom I was travelling spoke to an ancient man who was pressing grapes to make wine. The careworn villager, who told us that he had been making wine for many decades, deplored the paintings. He had prevented those of his own family members from being put up outside of his home. "They should dwell in our hearts, not on our walls," he said.

‽

We walked the uneven streets. Another of our Spanish fellow travellers, our host, said that there were almost no children living in Mogarraz. At the end of the village, many of the homes were boarded up. Crooked planks covered undersized doorways, centuries old. For sale signs were hand-painted, but they were hung without much conviction. The construction of the buildings was mixed. Wood frames were filled in with stones and then plaster. More recent plumbing pipes jutted out from some walls. Buildings were crumbling and untended. I thought that it would be a great place for a writing retreat, but that I wouldn't be able to live there. I chided myself for the thought. Back on the main street, some visiting children were rolling down the cobbles on bicycles. One girl of about ten yelled at us to clear the path. Older residents gathered in doorways or looked out from the windows above. They didn't have balconies. In some places, one could reach from a building on one side of the street to touch the building on the other. There were few shops, and none for tourists aside from the ham shop on the road on which we had arrived. A door opened onto a small bookshop run by a stooped man who was perhaps eighty or perhaps fifty. It was hard to tell. The shop receded into dim light, a hodgepodge of used titles aging into the dust behind. The poetry books, on a rotating rack, were given prominent display near the door. The shopkeeper and I nodded to one another as our group passed. At length, we reached the town's end. We looked over the valley below to the next village, listening to the quiet. Then we headed back into our cars and back to Salamanca, driving through a countryside of oaks and acorns.

⅄

In Peter Wohlleben's *The Hidden Life of Trees*, he states that a forest is like a superorganism in which the trees communicate with one another across the soil. The forests earlier in the day had seemed lush as they spread across the valleys. Yet the soil on the drive back to the city seemed weak. The coppiced trees were a long-standing monocrop. The fields had cattle but sparse evidence of people. Even though the city of Salamanca has grown considerably in the last century, the region still maintains a roughly equivalent population as it urbanizes and modernizes. The fields appeared to be lying fallow and untended. The farms were blinking out or being amalgamated, just as they were back home. I listened to the beautiful day and to the wind generated by our passage. I felt the sort of sad contentment that comes with witnessing the passage of time. In the evening we returned to the Plaza Mayor in Salamanca. In it, the roundel of Franco had been scratched out from the sequence of images of the previous rulers of Spain, a long line of stern-looking kings and queens. The other images were intact. The square was lit in warm yellows and children were out late. We took a small dinner off the square and went early to bed.

⅄

The next day on that trip I returned to Madrid on my own. Madrid is a space that puts into relief, for me, all of my thinking of St. Augustine, of Alberta and of the temporality of listening. I visited the Museo Nacional Centro de Arte Reina Sofía. I stood for a long time in front of Picasso's *Guernica*. I enjoyed the passing crowds recoiling at the horror of the painting, its sheer energy, just as I recoiled in turn. I studied Picasso's preparatory sketches for the massive, iconic canvas. Works by Joan Miró, Georges Braque, Fernand Léger, Francisco Goya, Dorothea Tanning and more hung throughout the gallery. There were many impressive paintings, mostly by men. The twentieth century, the horror of Spanish religious painting giving way to the horror of the Spanish experience of the century, its war and fascism. Films by Luis Buñuel were installed in some rooms. A recording of Kurt Schwitters's *Ursonate* played in a loop in another. Later I sat in Plaza de Juan Goytisolo in front of the museum. I had a salad of greens, tomatoes and mozzarella, as well as some clear and effervescent Spanish beer. The sun shone and spiders were ballooning on the breezes. I could see their billowing threads floating up and over the museum. Beautiful people passed by. The women were much better dressed than the men. A man crashed his bicycle going over a step. He came up bloodied and disoriented. He stepped into the restaurant to clean up. I thought about sound, music and noise, and how the museum that I was looking at used sound in its exhibits. I thought about the proximity of both the past and the present in the museum and on the street. I listened to the sounds around me. I could hear conversations in Spanish, English and French. Someone dropped into German for a moment, then back into Spanish. A woman came through the terrace, begging. She was shooed off by the servers. She came back as soon as the servers' backs were turned. Then she was shooed off anew. She seemed to have little to lose and ignored the servers as much as she could. Closing my eyes, I considered what I could hear, trying to tune my ears to the environment. Birds – sparrows – chirruped in the maples in the square. The maples, in turn, provided shade for my table. They were a different type of maple than the ones I normally see. The same is true for the flora in Spain in general: I am not used to it. I know many of the plants back home. They ground me, keep me grounded. The sun seemed to hang in the sky. Conversations buzzed and ice cubes clinked in glasses. From a block over, the noise of cars filtered into the square. Bicycles and then a skateboard, then a fluttering of pigeons. Smoke puffed from cigarettes, but that made only the smallest of sounds. People spoke into their mobile phones and a woman laughed. Spanish politics were in a poor state – the country had been suffering from a decade of austerity. On the train into Madrid, I had been struck by the sadness of the replanted forests, the pine trees clustered together on thin soils. There were few birds. One of my Spanish friends said that she had only once seen a deer in Spain. The environment around the city felt depleted. I listened anew to the sounds of the square. When I paid my bill, the machine said *espere por favor*. That is what the machines say in Spain. Literally, it means "wait, please," but etymologically it also means "hope, please."

⸎

While in Spain, I was also able to witness spaces and gaps that show me what is at stake in Alberta. From the presence of the historical record – so often devalued in Calgary, which too often bulldozes the past to make way for the shiny and new – to the different skies, the contrast is marked. From the dining-room table in the rented apartment in Salamanca on the darkened winter evenings, I wrote through these travels as a way of understanding what it means to listen to Alberta, what it means for me to listen to the land.

⸎

When I was in Madrid, I looked for quiet and green spaces. I walked away from the traffic noise of central Madrid. I entered the city park known as El Retiro, which I suppose signifies that it is a place to retire from the bustle. I sat next to the water and enjoyed an espresso and *churros y chocolate*, watching runners cross the park. An old man rowed a dory on the water. People gathered on the steps. There were green parrots flying about the trees. They chattered to each other. My boots were dusty from my travels. I watched. Walking down the broad boulevard of the park, people yelled into their mobile devices. Other mobiles emitted tinny sounds. A couple, man and woman, walking arm in arm, each yelled into a separate device, their faces turned away from one another. It wasn't a very musical scene, but it was a comical one. Others wore earbuds and listened to distant sounds. There were dog walkers. I veered my noticing between the shoes, the small size of the dogs and the overall din. Farther down the park I came to the Palacio de Cristal, the Glass Palace, which is now part of the art gallery. There was a display of some sort of glassworks. More impressive, however, was the building itself. It was a steel-and-glass edifice of the late nineteenth century. On that day, sunlight streamed high overhead. People walked around the building and it reverberated with their conversation as well as the constant twittering of birds. Two helicopters buzzed overhead, a loud whirring of blades cutting the air. A school group entered the building. Many people – young women in particular – were taking photographs of themselves in the space. The quality of the light was good, but better still was the sound, which the cameras could not capture. The voices bounced upward across the vaulted glass ceiling, lifting toward the sunlight. The tile work and archways complemented the clarity of the glazing. I left the building, wandered the park and found myself sitting with my back to a chestnut bough. I listened to the birds, the voices and the coughing of an old man. Nearby was a mixture of trees: pines, maples, chestnuts, palms and cedars of Lebanon. Three people practised yoga together, facing each other in a triangle next to a tall maple. Music played over a small portable speaker, guiding their movements.

⟨

When I am in different places, I contemplate how to situate the sounds in relation to the land on which I dwell. I wrestle with how to connect them to the mood of the moment in which we live, one that is sometimes scary, sometimes beautiful. Seeing the generations of Spanish modifications to the landscape prompts me to wonder about the future of the landscapes that I know well, close to home. Spain was, after all, one of the world's colonizing powers, even if not of the lands on which I live. At home, too, what Rob Nixon calls "slow violence" is around us every day as the numbers of bees, birds, butterflies and beyond dwindle around us while the world's poorest and most vulnerable suffer. Income disparity increases while Jeff Bezos and Elon Musk get richer. In my personal circles, I am seeing many people do the best that they can to give hope for the next generation on the backs of their own uncertainty. The pandemic puts all of these issues into stark relief. The United States is burning and Canada mustn't pretend that it doesn't share the same problems. I worry very much about my children's futures. Scrambling over diminishing job prospects and forced into social compliance due to the need to secure the next temporary contract, people lash out at one another. Fear drives people apart. What might bring us together? The anger out there has been redefining how we behave. This situation is cataclysmically dangerous at a time when we need to alter how we live in the world – if we want the world to continue to tolerate our species. How can any of that be heard on a quiet day in a park in a busy city in Spain, not long before the pandemic set in?

෴

When the pandemic did set in, I was forced to leave Spain quickly. At first, we were uncertain as to how much the new virus would affect the country. And then it hit. I came back through Madrid on the first night of the city's lockdown. The usually vibrant city was quiet, deserted. The intercity train came into the station as the sun set. I took a second train to the airport in the darkness. The train was empty. It was disquieting to be the sole passenger. The screens that told the riders which station came next were glitching. The computer system that ran them attempted to restart, but kept failing and then trying to restart anew. I had no idea whether I was on the right train or where I might end up. At length, however, I arrived. I slept fitfully in an airport hotel, and then took what ended up being the second-last commercial flight from Spain to Canada. At Madrid-Barajas Airport, the cavernous terminal was darkened and hushed. Most of the gates were empty and silent. Yet many people were attempting to board the same flight as I was, including many United States citizens who had been stranded by newly closed borders. They hoped to get to Canada and then find a way back home. The flight itself, though packed, was uneventful. I fell into my bed in Calgary exhausted by what became the early stages of the pandemic.

⸘

Listening to Simon and Garfunkel's "The Sound of Silence," yet again I am struck by the persistence of the anxiety that listening is a rare commodity. After I returned from Spain, I sat alone in my house for two weeks. I faced an early quarantine when we didn't know what the world held in store for us. Everyone else decamped for the time of my self-isolation in case I had brought the virus back home with me. During that time, I listened to the world change. I revisited old books and music. I was waiting and on edge. In Simon and Garfunkel's song, it is a matter of listening in order to sing. "The Sound of Silence" is a song that I like to belt out, bringing its lyrics to the front of my mind, even if my vocal range is not up to the task. My old, well-used record of the song is scratchy. The wobble of the uneven vinyl soothed me, though, more than the clear, digital version could have. I heard the fear expressed in the song about losing the ability to listen in the hurly-burly of busy, urban lives alongside the song's more explicit fear about loss. What are the sounds of silence? Unchecked, silence enlarges, but the remedies are there in the understorey, against the flashing neons and shouting of civic strife. The out-of-the-way places, the unrecognized places, are where the poetry is to be found, the song tells us. The question is in part whether anyone will hear the songs or read the words. The song is both a lament for lost voices – songs that are unsung – and a plea for audience and for listening. In the intervening years since that song was released, perhaps more of us have found a voice. Or have claimed one – to echo Adrienne Rich's moving terms in her address to the second wave feminist movement. This claiming of a voice is a laudable thing. But in the meantime, the witnessing, the listening that "The Sound of Silence" invites seems to be diminished. What, literally, is the sound of silence? It reads like a Zen koan. Yet I believe that I have witnessed it, on cold nights far from the city, when I am away from the jetsam of airplanes and the flotsam of electricity lines. That silence is not silence as such, but rather deeply full of sound, noise and contentment. I have to voyage farther and farther afield in order to find it. Or I have to search inward, more and more, into the remains of ruptured communities of care and compassion. To me, this shift, this loss of silence, is lamentable. Perhaps I glimpsed it from the empty house during my quarantine. The roads fell silent as the pandemic brought the world to a standstill. Human sounds diminished. Later, they resumed. What do we lose when we can no longer hear the sounds of silence?

{

It is not always an easy thing to listen to the land. We hear a world in pain, a world that is wounded. I try to describe it as best I can, though many days I feel that I am failing. Yet I try. I look for the beauty and resilience in the injured land. I think of Calgary's Shepard Landfill, where one of my children went on a field trip. It's a place that I have visited many times. I love its complexity. You may say that it seems odd to love the dump, yet I do. For all of its mixed-up, foul-smelling ways, I feel affection for the dirt, the grit, the rusted-out fridges, the decaying electronics, the puddles of orange water. The dump is loud – it has volume, it has heft, it has weight. It has nails, screws, broken glass that puncture tires, even the beefy tires of the old Chevrolet half-ton pickup that we used to drive when I worked in landscaping. What noise! The seagulls – Franklin's, Bonaparte's gulls – wheel overhead, squawking. The Caterpillars crush the waste. The trucks back up. The people yell at each other: "Look out!" Everyone should visit the dump. It is horrible and wonderful.

}

One time, when I must have been sixteen or seventeen, we found an abandoned cat at one of the dumps in Calgary. I had heard, listened, to a soft mewling that came from under a pile of garbage. We were hauling yard waste from someone's house. The cat was dirty, starving and scared. We scooped it up, into the truck, where it hid under the seat, scratching anyone who tried to coax it out. The cat ended up on its way to the humane society and then to wherever it ended up thereafter. I still hear the mews cutting through the grind of machines, the crushing and crunching of metal and glass. That crunching was the sound that I heard, too, the summer I worked at the recycling depot. The endless shattering of glass is still sticky and glistening in my memory. The dump, the depot are places where we can hear the volume of our wanton destruction. It is where we can hear, in the quiet under-rhythms of the earth's heartbeat, how we have created a world of suffering. It is a pain to which it is worth listening as a step toward healing our own broken hearts. The pain is everywhere. Yet it need not consume us if we are willing to hear it.

}

The old dump in my family's hometown of Athabasca was another site where I saw this complexity. It was on the south side of the river. Now there is a drop-off on the north side. I went to the old dump with my grandfather, driving into town. The box of the pickup was filled with the sorts of rubbish that couldn't be composted, or reused, or burnt in the oil drum behind the farmhouse. The trees surrounded the site. It was striking, there alongside the banks of the river.

≀

The side of the river matters. A book of local history produced out of Richmond Park, which is the rural area on the north side, bears the title *Reflections from Across the River: A History of the Area North of Athabasca*. It is a book steeped in listening, a massive documentary tome, produced as part of a rush of similar local history books. This one was written and edited by locals, and my maternal grandmother, Grandma June, consulted on it. The title of the book assumes a standpoint on the south side of the river, hearkening across to the north side from whence the reflections come. The land that does the witnessing seems to be the south side. The book implies that the south is the side of vision, of hearing, of reason and of civility. The document arrives out of the bush, attesting to its perseverance and endurance in all seasons, just like the grit of those who live there. The voices whispered across the water implore a listener on the other side. So many of the northern metaphors are metaphors of voice, sound and space. Athabasca is the Land of the Whispering Hills. Even a concept like the north implies a relationship. What does *north* mean? North of where? From whose perspective? Those from farther north with whom I have spoken find my understanding of the north laughable. It should more rightly be called another middle, except that it lies north of where most humans are – most people in Canada, but also most of the globe's human inhabitants. North indicates something spatial and temporal, a disjuncture with the not-north, whether or not we agree as to where north is. So you have to whisper and listen, strain your ears to hear the voices from across the river, over the bridge. When moving into the north, take a gentle reminder that perspective determines much, if not all, of what we are able to hear and to witness.

⁊

I imagine myself heading back to Athabasca. I listen to the car's speakers, old country music twanging from track to track as we drive north. We drive north from Calgary on Highway 2. As we go, we pass towns, small cities. Strip malls, car dealerships, larger malls. They have recently built a mall next to the mall. No really. There are light industrial patches for equipment, machine tooling. All of this land was once farmland. All of this land was once grassland, prairie, parkland, Indigenous land. It is a land of ongoing Indigenous presence. We pass farmland: canola, wheat, barley, oats. The crops gather the fumes from the SUVs tearing up the highway. Particulates move into our food chain. Still, the farmlands stretch out. I watch for hawks, maybe even owls, sitting on fence posts. Cattle are common, as are horses. There is an elk farm. There is an alpaca farm. All of this land is governed by treaties – 7, 6, 8 is the geographical order when one heads from south to north. Why aren't there signs to let us know when we cross treaty lines? There are signs for each county – Rocky View, Mountain View, Red Deer, Lacombe, Ponoka, Leduc. After Leduc, we skirt the city of Edmonton. There is a ring road now. The old way we used to go went past West Edmonton Mall, though there was another way that took about the same amount of time. We drive across the bridge over the North Saskatchewan River. Trees, riverbanks and bridges. Then we round through St. Albert, past new subdivisions eating up the topsoil. Then north. Farms, towns, then boreal forest. The whole drive has maybe a half-dozen grain elevators visible now. They are largely forgotten. They were once the cornerstone of every agricultural community. In another time, long ago, I learned how to work one. As I drive I watch the trucks. They are fast. They get dirtier, too, the farther north one goes. They are used for what they were designed for: dirt roads, gravel roads, no roads. At Westlock, we turn east; then, at Clyde, let the road wend north again. From here, at about the four-hour mark or so, and for the rest of the drive – the last hour or so – there is a wide shoulder and a large easement along the side of the highway, then trees. Only the occasional field pokes through. The trees are poplars, aspens, birches, spruces and pines. Willows edge into the mix. Granny taught me that the trees cycle over time, deciduous giving way to conifer. I look to see. Can I tell the difference now? Are there more spruces and pines than there were before? I watch the power lines. Trace them with my eyes as they dip, peak and then dip again with each pole.

⁘

The map is different in every season. In summer, it is lush, green-brown, insects buzzing and flying in the air. Mosquitoes give way to butterflies give way to grasshoppers and dragonflies. All of them end up squashed in the grills and on the windshields of trucks. So do too many deer and porcupines and skunks. Don't scratch the bug bites, especially June to August. Farther north and you start to hit the blackflies. In the fall, there are beautiful, golden, dying leaves and grasses, unless the snows come early. Tractors, combines and trucks are hard at work to get the crops in. The roads are slowed down by farm equipment. There aren't many roads to share. Winter arrives and there is the turnoff to the secondary highway, the one on which my aunt died in a car accident. I have passed that road many times. Black ice is always a risk. The snow covers the fields through the trees. It clings to the conifers when it falls wet and heavy. One might spot a snowy owl. I have seen one, once, on a fence post. The roads are snowy, icy. Snakes of snow blow along the blacktop, their white tongues gusting above the highway's ribbons of tarry patches. Driving early means being on the roads before the snowplows clear the way. Make sure that your vehicle is equipped. It should have blankets, flares, food, water. Spring, when it comes, is a time of melting. The green is brighter, the flowers spring up along the shoulders of the roads and the cows finish calving. The snow, crusted over, hangs onto the hollows and shady patches. Newborn animals stand up and shake themselves off. Round a bend, pass the truck dealerships and arrive in town.

⁂

The town is nestled in a valley amidst the trees, the boreal forest spread out around it. The Land of the Whispering Hills is an apt description. The hills are always whispering, leaves wrinkling in the sun and wind, snow blowing, insects calling. On all sides there are trees, water, hills. The trees end where the town begins, or perhaps it's the other way around. The road passes a motel, then the Inn and the industrial section of town – the United Farmers' of Alberta supply store, the utilities, the small oil and gas outfits. The road dips down, heading toward the river. It turns into Main Street. Main Street is Main Street. It is a small town, so there is no Walmart. We pass shops, services. First the fire hall, then the burger joint. There's a Chinese restaurant – one of several in town, though Kwan's was the first. A general store, then another, then a clothing store, then the banks. Main Street now has two traffic lights, up from zero when I was young. Not long after the first one went in, a truck smashed through a bank wall trying to stop for the lights in icy conditions. We might ponder what the "progress" of the new traffic light really meant. Down the hill, Main Street ends at the river, at the second light. Turn left or turn right. Left and toward the water is where the grain elevators used to be. Trains haven't run to Athabasca in a generation now. It used to be the last stop of the line. Instead, there's a grocery store and some historical nods to the trains and the grains that kept the town going as the fur trade receded. Up the hill, there's a garage, then a gas station, then the entrance to the university. (It's mostly just administrative buildings, as it's an online institution.) Then the road wends off toward farms, including those of some of my more distant relatives. The Hutterite colony is out that way too. But if we turn right at the second light, we pass the old brick hotel, the Union; then the liquor store – the one that used to be run by the province; then a campground and the old train crossing. From there, up the hill takes us to the newer section of town with the hospital, the newer elementary school and the water reservoir. From there the road heads into the forests, heading toward Amber Valley, an important historical settlement for Alberta's Black community. Amber Valley is a site of necessary stories, but ones that are beyond my capacity to record. The road passes the exit to the cemetery. Or turn left (via an underpass) and then drive past some businesses before getting to the bridge. Over the bridge, and our voice now joins those voices across the river, heading into patches of farmland that go into the forests, on the road that heads toward Calling Lake and the multiple parcels of the reserve lands of the Bigstone Cree Nation.

&

How should I write about this space and the lives lived in it? What is a narrative? What is music? I listen to the album *Deep Listening* by Pauline Oliveros, Stuart Dempster and Panaiotis. As I do so, I recognize evermore that the structure of music is never straight-forward. For her project, Oliveros descended into an underground cistern to record its sound. This changes how one might consider listening. It also challenges the human-centred nature of what music is often understood to be. That challenge, in turn, reflects back on narrative, on story. What if all of these – music, narrative and story – are somehow about land and how the land shapes us? The writing that I have taken on here wants words, it wants structure – but it also wants a poet's ear. The land itself is musical. But how does one grow a narrative? With a single growing season, one isn't likely to get all the way there. It needs careful attention. Seeds long since planted are growing now. They've become a tangled thicket out in the stand of trees behind the old outhouse. They need careful pruning in order to make sense on the page. What do we prune them into? A hedge? A maze? A part of me wishes to leave the tangle as it stands – it is part of the forest of my mind. To organize the thicket, encouraging some parts to grow while shearing others back, is to tame it, domesticate it, score it like a sheet of music. And yet, is story not also a way of finding order and reason within our windblown existences? I hold the bramble and the hedge in balance.

≀

If this is a narrative, then how to proceed in this work on listening? It's time to turn toward thinking about the people and the trees. Life in Alberta can be hard, cold and icy. It is not always easy – it is not always kind. At the same time, it can be communal, cheerful and ridden with laughter. Its landscapes are beautiful and often misunderstood. Perhaps it can be mapped, laid out and even comprehended. A map is a rendering of space, but also a representation of time. The planet is always in motion.

≀

I pause for a moment more, still stuck on this strange act of writing. Writing is, for me, one of the most pleasurable, grounding things. When I am writing, I am well, even if what I write ends up in the bin. When I write, I know where I am. (Ah-ha! Writing is a map.) I can locate myself and I can work through the challenges. Some writers will say that they hate the act of writing, but enjoy having written. I prefer the act of writing to the final result. I draft longhand, a liquid ink pen across an unlined page. The chicken scratch of my writing is not something even I can always decipher afterwards. I tried fountain pens. Being left-handed, however, those leave me making a mess of the page. I adjust, using a heavy enough paper stock to absorb the ink quickly and deeply. I write in short bursts, ten minutes or so at a time, after thinking for a long while. In the best-case scenario, these bursts happen early in the day. Even better if it's before I've been in front of any screens. I write most often surrounded by books. In the beforetime, before pandemic life, I was fond of writing in coffee shops. Yet I write well when I am far from others, too. I have written in small, off-the-grid cabins on islands on the west coast. I used to write in the shack behind my parents' old cabin in small-town Alberta, no phone or Internet in sight. The room in which I now write provides another map. I move between the dining-room table and the second-floor study that overlooks trees and a small courtyard. The room has a fireplace, two couches, bookcases built into the walls and the second dining-room table. Books of poetry are to my left, Brand-Carson-Cohen-Nichol. Philosophy and theory jostle one another, Butler-Chomsky-Foucault-Marx, to my right. Soon I will make myself an espresso, the one coffee that I allow myself each day in order to balance my nerves and my wakefulness. I'd be kidding if I said that this space was tidy. Laundry that wants folding is on the couch, empty glasses stand here and there, papers cram the table and the carpet needs vacuuming. But it is warm, it is quiet and it is home. I turn the page and put on more music.

II

We find speaking of the Anthropocene, even speaking in the Anthropocene, difficult. It is, perhaps, best imagined as an epoch of loss – of species, places and people – for which we are seeking a language of grief and, even harder to find, a language of hope.
– Robert Macfarlane, *Underland: A Deep Time Journey*

But the only people who hear the saints and philosophers are those who keep on listening.
– Robert Bringhurst and Jan Zwicky, *Learning to Die: Wisdom in the Age of Climate Crisis*

The second date written on the bottom of the dining-room table is 1988, when the table was rebuilt. This date is written in my father's handwriting. In that year, while we were living in Vancouver, he disassembled and reconstructed the table. He also made two leaves as inserts to expand it. These leaves were – and are – a near match to the original wood, though they have always left a very slight gap when they are put in. The dowel ends slot just a little bit unevenly into holes long-since drilled into the tabletop. I spent many an afternoon oiling the wood surface, especially once my parents gave the table to us for our growing household. They shipped it from Calgary all the way to Halifax, where we were living after my studies. It occupied pride of place alongside the wooden pressback chairs that my parents first acquired in Ontario in the 1970s. And then, only a few months later, we found ourselves moving back to Calgary and, as a result, shipped the table right back to the city from which it had come.

≀

One summertime, not long ago, I was driving my rusting, aging Mazda west on Calgary's 17th Avenue. Seventeenth Avenue has felt down on its luck of late, even before the pandemic. To me, though, it remains a central and in many ways well-heeled strip of the city. It houses a number of trendy restaurants, bars, nightclubs and shops. Some are still open, while other empty storefronts wait for the times to improve. On this particular summer day, it was full of life. It was a sunny afternoon and people came out of the woodwork to stroll the streets, people-watch and catch the warm sunshine. This was during the last oil boom. I ended up driving behind a Lamborghini. I don't recall its colour, nor its specific model, but I could peer into the wee rear window and see a youngish man behind the wheel. I have never seen anyone who wasn't a dude driving a Lamborghini. For the sake of what follows, let's say that the Lamborghini was blue. We drove along. The man was driving slowly, showing off his symbol of wealth and status. People looked at his shiny car. Then they looked past my clunky yet effective ride. We pulled up to a light. Just before the light changed to green, a car turned into our flow of traffic. It was another Lamborghini. Let's say that this one was yellow, but otherwise the same in all significant respects. It was driven by another youngish man. Presumably he had also been enriched by the boom. Presumably he was also unencumbered by many responsibilities.

Calgary was like this during the boom years, and it was particularly evident in the summertime. Expensive cars came out to enjoy the warmth, not unlike mosquitoes, wasps and other biting and stinging insects. We were now in a procession: yellow Lamborghini, blue Lamborghini and me in my Mazda. People looked at the Lambos. I nodded to an onlooker. I received a look of mild disdain in return. The Lamborghinis seemed uncomfortable, however. They started to weave a little bit in the lane, posturing, showing off. Then, as we went through an intersection, the blue Lamborghini peeled off, turning the corner with a loud engine roar. He did so in order to get out, I supposed, from under the shadow of the usurper: the newly arrived, yellow Lamborghini that had supplanted him at the head of the column. Fair enough. We drove on. The traffic was calm. The day was grand. A minute or two later, we passed another block. A car turned onto the road behind me. It was the same Lamborghini, the blue one. It must have driven around the next block in an attempt to get back into the lead, only to end up third in our revised parade: yellow Lamborghini, rusting Mazda, blue Lamborghini. We drove along in our glory. This time I waved to an onlooker. I got an enthusiastic, single-fingered wave in response. The Lamborghini motors hummed. My Mazda chugged. We left the main strip of 17th Avenue and I turned south. The story ends there. Calgary is no longer like this, but it was once. Many Calgarians are praying for the day when the Lamborghinis return in their former numbers. They are sifting the runes and reading the prophecies, hoping for a sign. Others among us are looking to the future, knowing that something else will be coming.

{

On another day, not long before the world turned, we were in Edmonton. The day was loud, crisp and sunny. Greta Thunberg stood on the steps of the legislature, sixteen years old, wearing a down jacket. "Can you see her?" I asked my kids. "I can see her eyebrows," one of them answered. It was only a few months before the pandemic. I didn't expect Thunberg to be carrying the same sign that I had seen in the pictures, but she was. It was on plywood, black text on white paint: *skolstrejk för klimatet.* After local organizers spoke – Indigenous people, people of colour, youth – Thunberg's turn came. Ten thousand people cheered. I had been rallying and protesting and marching in solidarity since the 1990s, starting with a rally against Alberta's then premier Ralph Klein's cuts to education, yet this was the largest demonstration that I had ever seen in this province. Thunberg's message was distinct. It rang out across the filled square, overtop of the few angry white men in the crowd. These men were outnumbered, it seemed, by a thousand to one. Later, they would be given airtime in the media in the name of including "both sides of the story." Listen, Thunberg said, and thank you. She acknowledged the territory, the Indigenous land keepers, and she was unmincing in her speech. Listen to science, she repeated. Listen to the youth. We cheered and spoke back to a relentless provincial government. I reflected on the scene, finding that I was giving up on my generation and investing my hopes in the young. My generation is proving itself to be inadequate to the challenge. Standing there, we focused on Thunberg's speech, not on the climate change denier behind us. My children held my hands, which is increasingly rare as they age. And then it was over. The crowd began to move. We found ourselves next to a police cordon of bikes. It had been set up in order to provide an exit from the podium. A human chain of young people formed around Thunberg. Then, all of a sudden, we were next to her. Her eyes scanned us, serious. She smiled and then thanked the reporter who had sidled up beside her. She was short, we observed, much shorter than any of us. What does it take to create a movement? How can one motivate a global audience? I lamented the cowardice of my age. I recognized a tiny shard of myself in the angry, aging white men. They felt that their way of life was under siege. In some ways, it is, because we cannot continue to live in the ways that we have done. I feel that tension too, if I am honest. It is not a feeling that I enjoy. I can see how I have been trying to build a safe life for my children. How I have hardened to my own contradictions in order to try to make their lives possible. Yet Thunberg was right on that day: the world is changing, it must change and it will change. The task is to learn to listen. If I do well, I might help to create a future that is not dominated by people who look like I do. Whatever might happen in the future, though, for the moment, Thunberg's message sufficed. And then she was gone. We cleared out of the grounds.

⁂

A few months later, just before I was forced to come home from Spain, I visited the village of Ledesma. I had been reflecting for a long time on what it might mean to live in an era defined by human impacts on the environment – an idea summed up by those who use the term *Anthropocene* to characterize this epoch. By then we were all watching the news reports of a new and ill-understood virus that was starting to spread rapidly. Ledesma is a small, now partly depopulated village not far from Salamanca. It is famous for raising bulls for the bullfights. The Romans knew it as Bletisa. A friend drove the two of us through Salamanca and across the countryside, past empty early March fields and groves of oaks, charting along the Río Tormes. Before long, the riverbed opened into a shallow gorge that was strewn with rocks. Small boulders dotted the landscape. The town was perched on top of a hill, where it straddled the river, with two bridges – the new, serviceable one and the older one. We crossed the river and entered the town centre. After seeking directions, we found the *taberna* where we had lunchtime reservations. We were late, the tavern keeper told us. She cheerfully ushered us in nonetheless through the low door. The restaurant was packed. It was a marked contrast to the almost deserted town outside. I stood out because I was a foot or so taller than most of the locals. All of the locals were aged. Youth seemed to be nowhere in sight. Every time that I turned in the tavern, the owners reached up to put their hands to my head to make sure that I didn't injure myself. It was welcome guidance, as the doorways were very low indeed. Even the ceiling was not much greater than my six feet. We sat in one corner of the small, full room. We ate a delicious meal. I had garlic soup (mostly meat), followed by a plate of excellently cooked pork. There were no side dishes or vegetables, just lots of meat. We had local red wine from a pitcher. I learned the practice of mixing it with soda water. Dessert consisted of flan and strong coffee that was brewed, the owners told us, with a charred bit of wood in it. Presumably the fiery brand gave the coffee a chicory sort of effect. As we finished the very cheap lunch – ten euros apiece – the owners showed us around. They took us to the back to see the fire on which they cooked; it was tended by an old woman. She insisted on showing us her swollen legs and the incision from when she had recently had her infected leg drained. The man of the house showed us around, displaying autographed photos of famous matadors. We thanked them and headed out. Then we drove up to the empty main square. It was topped by an enormous cathedral. Leaving the car there, we wandered the streets past old homes that had long since been bricked up in the hopes of better times to come. At length, we arrived at the town's castle. My host knew how to gain entrance and stepped into the bar next door to ask the bartender for the key. He handed it over to us so that we could tour the castle on our own. The castle was small, with a ground level and a rampart. From the rampart we surveyed the valleys in all directions. It was quiet. We were the only visitors. A soft rain began as we walked the castle walls. There was not much to see beyond the village falling into ruins, the ancient disused castle and a picturesque set of hills rolling into the distance. It was beautiful and solitary. As the rain gained momentum, we locked the castle back up and returned the key. We found our way back to the car in the main square and then drove back to Salamanca, listening all the way.

⁂

To listen well is also to listen for a long time and across many places. Historical listening; geographies of sound. I live in a place that is unlike Spain in so many ways. I live in a place, for instance, that loves to forget. Canada has a hard time remembering hardships. Remembering those means calling to mind injustices and wrongs that continue into the present. My province of Alberta is good at selective forgetting. We are currently enduring a government that seeks to roll back time to an imagined one that never existed. It was a supposed magical time when oil was great and everyone got rich off of extractive resource harvesting – not just the lucky few. It was perhaps some time in the 1950s or '60s, not too long after the Leduc oil strike of 1947. The provincial government is spending millions of public dollars to take the federal government to court, to support the oil and gas industry and to go to war with environmental groups that dare to use terms like *tar sands*. Or course the situation is complex. My point is that the government is nostalgically invoking a time that never really happened. My parents and grandparents lived in poor circumstances throughout that time, struggling to make ends meet on their farms. People in my family grew up without indoor plumbing, without electricity, well past the time when people living in cities could assume these regular amenities (which are, still, far from regular in all places). The idea that the past, the bituminous past, was a better one that should be revived at all costs does not fit this changing world. It also erases what life was like for poor Albertans even during the boom. Instead of that erasing and forgetting, I want to remember. I want to do so by listening. I am trying to listen to the voices that came before me – like the radical voices of the prairies: Mistahimaskwa (Big Bear), Louis Riel, the Famous Five, Tommy Douglas and so many others. All of them complex, imperfect figures who endeavoured to make the world a little bit better in the ways that they understood. There is so much potential in remembering to listen to these voices. Not in a conservative gesture to retell a reductive vision of the past, but instead to be guided by the potential that those voices contained – to build on them. What is the legacy of the Winnipeg General Strike one hundred years later? The Co-operative Commonwealth Federation, forerunner to the NDP, was founded in Calgary in 1932. What can we make of the movements of this place, when we remember them?

⸳

I am listening in order to remember and acting in order to try and honour those who came before. For instance: I am a jam maker because my father is a jam maker. He is a jam maker because his mother, Granny, was a jam maker. There is a line of us preserving fruits against the frozen winters, a line that crosses the Prairies and extends back – or at least so I imagine – to the steppes and highlands before. Jams and jellies on my paternal side, pickles on my maternal side. I hope to teach my children to be jam makers too. I learned from my father, whose jams are a bit more citified, a bit more twentieth century, than his mother's were. He uses commercial pectin and has been known to add colour to some jams so that they have the right technicolour pop. The jars of jam line up, glowing orbs, on late summer countertops. My parents have one of the few apricot trees in Calgary that provides fruit. It's rare in this environment, although Calgary has recently been redesignated as a warmer growing zone as the climate changes. The apricot tree doesn't provide much fruit, none at all most years, but when it produces, some years it has been enough to make jam. Granny's jams and jellies were more central to eating on the farm as I remember it. No food colouring, certainly. I'm not sure whether she added pectin. Jam thickens well on its own when cooked down, the natural fruit pectin taking care of the rest. Jars were sterilized in a bath of boiling water, then sealed with a layer of paraffin wax. I loved Granny's cold room, the room under the stairs in the basement of the farmhouse. It was a room where I never saw Grandpa Ken go. It smelled of potatoes and onions. There were pickles, yes, but above all jam. It was made from things that grew on the farm: wild strawberries, the enormous patch of raspberries, saskatoons from the bush and gooseberries. My favourite was the pin-cherry jelly made from fruit harvested off a tree near the raspberry canes, from out past the hole in the ground where the old farmhouse stood. Not far from the derelict outhouse and the boarded up old well. The jelly glowed red, sweeter than sweet, with a unique taste of its own. It was translucent and melted on bread, toasted or fresh, with or without peanut butter. I make my jam, I suppose, to honour Granny's.

ʒ

Granny died of brain cancer when I was fourteen, long before I had children of my own. The illness manifested in earnest shortly before her planned retirement from the elementary school in town. The town school was where she taught later in life – once her five boys were older, once her husband was sober – after a time of teaching on the Hutterite colony. I think of her when I make my own jams and jellies every year, starting when the strawberries ripen. My preserves are a compromise between the country version and the city version. I prefer windfall fruits, whatever is overflowing at any given moment. I gleefully accept the bounty of a friend's overrunning rhubarb patch, or a tree dropping plums faster than they can be eaten, or the deluge of marginal apples that fall in the autumn and make for good sauce. I sterilize jars in the oven and use store-bought pectin. Colouring, though, is a no go. Lids do the sealing rather than wax. The pop of a sealing jar remains one of my favourite sounds, a distinctive quick reversal of metal as the cooling jam and the air in the jar compress and shrink the space inside, forcing the convex lid into concavity.

ι

It took me many years to better understand Granny – really, to better understand everyone who has come and gone before me. A friend of mine tells me that our relationships with people continue well past their deaths. I know that he is right. My daily encounter with Granny's day planner already reminds me of that in its stains and wear. Years after her passing, after I took to reading – the option of being a popular kid proving elusive to me, leaving me to the friendship of books and of bookish friends – my grandfather let me choose from Granny's shelves before he got rid of their contents. It was the final time that I remember being on the farm. I was very conscious of the space left behind on each dusty shelf as I pulled down the volumes. Herbert Marcuse's *One-Dimensional Man*, Paulo Freire's *Pedagogy of the Oppressed*, Freud, local histories and a book called *Understanding the Female Orgasm*. It would take me many more years to reckon with these books and with what must have been the relative isolation of Granny's intellectual life, being a philosophical and thoughtful reader in northern Alberta's farming communities. I found, also, what may well have been the last book that she was reading, Thomas King's *Green Grass, Running Water*. It would have just been released in the paperback edition that I held in my hands. I was looking over the novel when I stumbled across what could have been her last notes, written directly on the rear flyleaf of the copy. Here is a typescript of what the note read:

> 2nd trip to hospital – can't retain
> fluids or food –
>   Fri July 15 / 94 to Atha. Municipal
> – Mol admitted me. Oldale on holidays
> July 16 / 94 shipped me on to Royal Alex in
> Edmonton for a CAT-test. Dr. Venderwande,
> Ross, ~~Đ~~ Neil, Dad, all came along. A tumor in
> rt temporal lobe – Today only treatment
> was ₐ steroid to reduce swelling. Scary stuff

Within a few months, Granny died after invasive and intensive procedures. I was able to visit a couple of times during her rapid decline. What strikes me about her note is its desire, on the one hand, to record events by date and by detail – and on the other hand, its quiet vulnerability. Granny's admission, at the note's end, of her fear. There was a bookmark in the middle of *Green Grass, Running Water*. The spine was uncracked after that page.

❧

Thomas King's *Green Grass, Running Water* remains one of my favourite books.

❧

What are the empty shapes left after we go? Our outlines on the bed, our presence in others' lives, the daily things that we did, ate, consumed. The people whom we loved, our touch on our lovers' skins. The plants that we watered and tended. The spaces that we inhabited. On that last trip to the farmhouse, not long before my grandfather sold it and moved into town and into his own retirement, I opened the door to the cold room once again. It had been years since my last visit. The potato smell was lighter now. There were fewer jars. It was dustier. What broke my heart was a row of four or five small, round, one-cup jars of pin-cherry jelly, their seals gone, mould overtaking what had once been inside. One of the last things that Granny had made, left to rot on a shelf. My anger at my grandfather for wasting it passed. Perhaps he had felt unable to eat it and to relinquish these final traces. I do not know. I beheld only the jars, no longer glowing orbs, their inner light long extinguished. So what are the shapes left empty after we go? Granny left a jam-shaped gap. I fill it each summer and fall with new fruit, listening for the pop of the lids to tell me and my children that she is still here.

≀

The old farmhouse, on the south side of town, was linked to my maternal side of the family on the north side of town by the bridge that spans the Athabasca River. I've believed for many years that that bridge is held up by nothing more than a few fingers. Let me explain. The bridge is old now. It's due to be replaced. It is an iron girder bridge, completed in 1952. The bridge may be iron and steel in its framing and spans, but its planking is wood. The wood is old: weathered boards, wide-cut and worn such that the knots and the grain in the wood stick up. Surely the wood has been replaced multiple times. Yet the wear is merciful, because the wood grain provides traction in the winter, especially during freeze-up, when heavy steam-fogs lift from the water and settle on the deck. Before the bridge, crossing was harder. In the summer there was a short ferry ride that you could take on a little barge, reminiscent of the times when sternwheelers used to land on the flats. A cable car could also transport you across the water from above, but it couldn't bear much weight. So if you lived on the north side of the river, as my maternal family did, it meant that medical emergencies were very real. When the river was impassable, one either had to be sent out by cable car into town for treatment, or else the doctor had to come across. Babies were born by midwife – one of my great-grandmothers, I am told, delivered the babies in the area. It's likely because of this time before the bridge that some residents still think of north of the bridge as being the edge of civilization. It marks the beginning of an otherworldly zone away from town.

⸮

Services were patchy north of the bridge. When phone lines arrived after the bridge opened, they were party lines, and everyone in the district could listen in on your phone calls. The few settlers in Richmond Park – the rural district north of the bridge, which is supposed to have been given its name by my Polish great-grandfather for no good reason of which we are aware – were few and far between: remote Ukrainian, Polish, French and Anglo-Scots farmers. The Cree lived – and live – on the reserve at Calling Lake, farther to the north, and beyond. As for those fingers? They once belonged to the writer George Ryga, whose controversial play *The Ecstasy of Rita Joe* helped to bring Indigenous issues to the ears of settler Canadians in the late 1960s. According to my grandmother, Ryga was one of the workers who had helped to build the bridge and he lost several fingers in an accident. His biography, which I read much later, confirmed it. The Ryga farm was just up the road from my maternal family farm. The story goes that Ryga lost his fingers in a concrete pouring accident on a cold winter's day, but I never thought of it quite like that. George Ryga has now passed on after living most of his life in the Okanagan Valley in British Columbia. His novels set in the region of his youth are too often forgotten. Yet the bridge stands, and I imagined for the longest time that it did so only because of those missing fingers, stuck between two spans, dextrously holding it all in place.

ƥ

As a child, I loved the bridge. I still love the bridge. In town, the river is muddy, wide and slow-moving. It eddies along, breeding mosquitoes at its margins. The bridge is wide too, the spans of rusty iron girders suspending the wooden deck with its worn boards. From the shoreline downtown, the bridge is off to the right. From the bridge itself, you can get a good, if brief, view of town. The bridge seems to be two lanes wide, but no painted line divides it. There are scrapes along the guardrails that show the colours of the paint of the pickups that have drifted too close. As a child, I loved crossing the bridge in the winter in particular, when the ice fogs clambered up from the riverbed. The safest way to cross is to treat the bridge as a single lane, to wait until there is space to drive across it alone. I recall the feel of soft tires rolling, *glomp glomp glomp*, along the knots, the ice in between the knots floating the car toward the rails like a needle in a groove. I still feel with that child's vision, hear with that child's ear. Looking out the window, ten-year-old me could see the night sky above the fog, the expanse of space stretching out, the snow, the spruces, the birches, the stars, the stars and the stars.

ƥ

North of the river meant returning to the bush – even if the divide between "bush" and civilization gives us pause because we know that nothing is ever that simple. North of the river is where half of my family comes from. If my mother hadn't been able to take that school bus every day over the bridge and across the Treaty 8 and Treaty 6 divide and into town, my parents would perhaps never have met. For that, I must thank George Ryga for his sacrifice. Mom's farm was on the north side, the side of the forests, the lakes, the moose, the bears and what to the southern imaginary remained the unknown. Her father hunted for some of their food. They ate what was available, from deer and moose right up to bear meat, which they did once end up eating. My grandparents hired people from local Cree communities to help on the farm. One time they came to stay in tipis across the farmyard. My grandfather spoke English, Polish and some Cree as a result. Aside from English, the dominant one in which I write to you, these are languages that my family has lost. The family relied on steady well waters. There were fires, there was death, there was life, warmth behind frozen doors and the blankets nailed to the door frames and frozen there, along with every loss and love.

{

Among the losses were the odd digit here and there, like Ryga's missing fingers. It's worth noting that such absent digits were not very remarkable in the context of northern Alberta life at the time. Men especially were often missing fingers – or more – as a result of farming or construction accidents. When I was growing up, I was around such fingerlessness often enough. I think of my paternal grandfather's best friend, who had had most of one of his hands crushed in an accident. Or I think of John, the old farmhand to my maternal grandparents. He had lost the ring finger on one hand, a loss suitable to his status as a roughened, lifelong bachelor who lived in a shack across the farmyard when my mother was growing up. I was terrified by these men's missing fingers. John liked to scare me by displaying the gap where his finger should have been. For years I thought about how best to write about the ways in which labour quite literally calls for bodily sacrifice. The body itself used up, piece by piece, in the quest for money or just for survival. The hardscrabble settling of northern Alberta took such tolls, though I have witnessed it in working peoples' lives everywhere that I have lived or travelled.

ξ

As a child, Grandma June, my maternal grandmother, drove me around town and over the bridge. Grandma was local to this landscape. She was a teacher before she married and then laboured on the farm and raised her family until her husband passed away some years before my birth. She drove a boat of a car by the time I came along, a blue Mercury Cougar with two bench seats with old grey lap belts. I loved the sound of the engine, the smell of the interior. It had an automatic gearshift on the wheel and a radio that I cannot ever recall being turned on. The radio was all fascinating dials and knobs. While I drove more often with Granny, Grandma's car made more of an impression. Granny drove daily from the farm to her teaching job in a little old Toyota Tercel. She taught me how to drive in that car. Driving lessons were the only time I ever heard her swear. I was behind the wheel of the car, rolling backwards at a stop sign toward a large pickup, when a four-letter word crossed her lips. Granny was adept, zipping around in her wee hatchback. With Grandma, on the other hand, it felt like we roamed out to visit extended family, or that we meandered to the grocery store. We drifted in that ample car. When going down hills – especially the hill down from the new part of town to the valley – she would put the car in neutral in order to save on gas. The car was loud, the engine assertive. It was suited, oddly, to the roads of the north. So many stories that I heard as a child ended with fishing cars out of snowbanks. Front-end winches remain recommended gear for a northern Alberta pickup. My family has had a long history driving those roads. One time, long after her death, I found my great-grandmother's driver's licence in

Grandma's house. Driver's licences weren't issued in Alberta until 1929, long after driving had already become a standard practice. The number of my great-grandmother's licence was very low, something like #27.

⁊

Of all the sites in town, the dump really was one of my favourites when I was young. I passed over it too fast earlier on, when I was mapping out the place. The old dump was right next to the bridge, not far from where Grandma and I would drift down the hill toward downtown and the river. I never went to the dump with Grandma, because she lived in town by the time that I was a kid and had town services, like garbage pickup. Granny and Grandpa, however, had no service from the farm. As much as possible, they saved and re-used whatever waste they had. They composted their food waste. They also had occasional garbage fires in an old oil drum out behind the farmhouse. Doing so seemed normal to me as a child. I still don't find it all that off-putting. What couldn't be reused, compost-ed or burned was saved for trips to the dump. I went on a few of these, riding along in the cab of the pickup while the box of the truck carted along whatever waste needed to be hauled. Entering the dump meant a hello to the men who ran it. Then one sorted whatever one brought. That dump had a small landfill and sorting station, but it's now closed. Instead there is a recycling and waste site across the river, on the north side, and a landfill fifty kilometres out of town. The old dump was surrounded by trees and was, to me, a bright, cheerful place filled with the castoffs of life. My feelings about landfills are inevitably warm. I think of the sounds of crush-ing cans, smashing glass and the engines of machinery. The treads of bulldozers breaking wood and waste. I feel revulsion at human behaviour, yet awe at how we manage this system. I think of that old landfill: the sounds of birds wheeling overhead, the murmur of the pickup, my grandfather's hands hucking trash into the tip. I am somehow happy at the memory.

⁊

My grandfather, as I knew him, was a gruff and melancholy, yet at times warm, man. He was short on words in most of our interactions. He was also quite deaf and only got hearing aids late in life. But his silence was much more than that. It was, I believe, a silence born of a personal suffering that I could not understand. He was a farmer, beset by the woes and anxieties that farmers have faced for a long time in Canada. In later years, the farm began a transition toward becoming one of the first organic farms in northern Alberta. As far as I know, it never quite got there. But my grandparents tried. Grandpa Ken also worked in oil and gas exploration, part of a seismic crew. He spent winters in the far north, when the farm was under a thick coat of ice and snow. There he lived in camps, performing tests to seek oil and gas formations deep underground. My grandfather was a tough man, a man who once killed a polar bear with a bow and arrow. A man who, another time, saved another worker from a polar bear mauling. A man who, in yet another tale, once kicked a polar bear through a doorway as it tried to get into the kitchen in the crew's trailer. All of these stories, though, were ones that I heard second-hand, not from him. His sons told the stories, while he preferred to work in the garage. Finally, my grandfather was an alcoholic, though he was sober by the time that I knew him. AA turned his life around. He was devoted to the meetings and the roundups – the gatherings of the AA community. AA gave him a social net in his later years. Before then, he nearly lost it all to his addiction. But that part of his story comes before my experience of him. While the family was always open about his being in AA, what brought him there is much less mine to share. Some stories are perhaps best honoured by being held in the past. We could have a lengthy debate about that proposition, however. One in which I would likely disagree with myself.

⁊

The lost digits and limbs of lives spent working in harsh conditions show up in so many of the stories. I return to Grandpa Ken's tales. I learned to play cribbage and to drive a tractor from him, though I don't recall spending a lot of time at his knee. But I learned much more along the way. My memories are of cigarette smoke, of his riding the tractor across the farmyard, or of his tools, the garage in which he was forever fixing broken pieces of machinery. Plaid mackinaws, snowy workboots. The sound and smell of his pickup trucks. As a farmer, he worked long hours, spring to fall, in an effort to make a go of farming in a difficult environment. But in the winter slowdowns he went north. So, in the winters, Granny and her sons oversaw the farm. They managed as best they could. In the north, my grandfather worked for the same company for over thirty years. He was involved in setting, detonating and measuring seismic charges. Grandpa and the crew would be left in a trailer with supplies and would blow up things underground, listening for the reverberations. The photos that survive from that time show some rough-and-tumble men from many places. They enacted their manhood in an environment of snow and ice, snowmobiles and diesel generators. No way in or out but by air or the ice roads. People got bushed. The stories from the far north also feature lost digits. And frozen bodies. As his sons told the stories, Grandpa would sometimes be there to grunt or interject a correction. Perhaps a correction to the story of the man who, out walking in the northern bush in the winter, tripped and managed to sever his own nose by landing on his machete.

⁊

In Grandpa's stories I heard the sound of long winter nights, the cold and natural threats out-of-doors. There was laughter at near misses that had been survived. I imagined the noise of bears snuffling. I listened for the details. The stories where my grandfather could, for a brief spell, play the role of hero were the ones that I thought best. Especially against bears. The bear that wouldn't leave the camp's garbage midden – the bear that Grandpa dispatched – was a good story, for example. I found most striking the story of the time that Grandpa and the crew woke to discover that one of their bunch was missing. The man had gone out in the night to relieve himself. They found him, mauled and nearly frozen, not far from the trailer. Yet the bear had left him alive. In the story, my grandfather helped to bring him in and then got under the blankets with the man, slowly warming him back to life, as one must do for victims of hypothermia. I do not know the outcome beyond the fact that the man lived. I imagine that he was airlifted out by bush plane. It would serve the story well if the man lost his toes or his fingers, but those details were never part of the narrative that I heard. What impressed upon me, and from a young age, was the cost of labour, the work that asked for small pieces of bodies, bodies left in fragments by the elements, by the cold, by the cold costs of just living.

ĝ

There is an unsorted box of photographs from that time, the 1960s and 1970s, in my parents' house. Photography, then, took much more effort and care. So I take note of what appears in the pictures. Farms, farm animals – cows, horses and dogs, mostly – and family gatherings, smiling collections of my forebears and their neighbours. In one memorable shot, a woman – no one can remember who she was – is standing on two moving horses, one foot in a stirrup of each, smiling at the camera. Then there are pictures of the far north. These photos mean that my grandfather took a camera with him on at least some of the trips. There are photographs of vast expanses of ice and snow – sunny, cold, brittle environments that I cannot place. I anticipate that he spent at least some time near Cape Dorset, as he brought home lithographs by Inuit arists from that region, as well as carvings. Two lithographs by the artist Pudlo hang in my parents' home. There are photos of the trailers in which the camp men stayed. Some interior shots of the men at rest. There are some shots of my young grandfather – at about the same age that I am now – looking less beaten and worn down by the world, by the weight of irresolvable finances, lost calves, failed crops and drink. There are photos of the machinery that they were using: snowcats and snowmobiles, plows, drills and things that I cannot identify.

{

I have understood little of Grandpa's life up north. I have seen it as one of the gaps between us. Yet the seismic work that my grandfather was a part of, I realized through conversations with others, was also a form of listening to the land. The data that the early crews were generating involved laying a field of instruments linked to a blasting cap. When the detonation went off, equipment recorded the vibrations and used these in order to show the different densities of what lay below. Doing so allowed the teams to map the subterrane, because oil, gas, rock and ice deposits have different densities. They send back different vibrational responses to the blasts. The same crews came back winter after winter and the experienced teams became proficient at laying charges well and generating solid data. I found myself thinking of Michael Ondaatje's novel *In the Skin of a Lion*. I recalled the father at the beginning of that book is a dynamiter hired by logging companies to clear jams along waterways. Expertise in blowing stuff up is valuable. Knowing how to listen to the land, to ice, to trees, and then knowing how to move them efficiently is a thing that is valued. And those on the land are the ones doing the work of listening, too, even while that very act of listening may be in the service of labour that may harm the land. It is perhaps a paradox: those who live closest to the land, whose livelihoods are linked to altering and even perhaps injuring it, also often have the best understanding of it – how to care for and steward it, if only they are given the chance. When people who live in rural environments express distaste for urban environmentalists – who have little experience with or connection to the land – I find myself more and more understanding their displeasure.

≀

The photographs of the north are cold, desolate. The colours are accentuated by the old Kodachrome film stock. I imagine the frozen earth under my smoky grandfather's feet rumbling. The equipment listens to the vibrations. Another day's work complete. There are photos taken of happy faces inside the trailer. Men lounge in their long johns and flannel shirts. Cards lie on the table. Cigarettes are being smoked down to their filters. It's a limited supply. Dynamiters, technical crews, engineers, cooks, cleaners. The equipment is out there, freezing. The nights are long and cold. The stars grind overhead and the music of the northern lights shimmers. I try to imagine the numbing cold, day after day, and the repetition of those days and nights on the land. As someone who seldom deals with quite so flat a geography, nor quite such an expanse of time, the prospect is both thrilling and terrifying. I think of how humans listen to one another, listen to the land, endeavouring to negotiate our complex relationships with one another, as I look over these old photos of the icy distances.

≀

I have recently received my paternal grandparents' silverware in the mail from one of my uncles. I said that I would be happy to be the keeper of this piece of the family's story, committed as I am to honouring those family members who have come before, as well as the hardships that they endured. For all of their strengths and faults – their goodness and their failures – they are the reason that I am able to sit here today at the table and write. The silver is monogrammed and comes in a felt-lined wooden box, which is painted with a dark patina on top of the decorative bevel work. It is old, chipped, worn and stained. The top panel of the box is delaminating in one corner. The buffeted wood, though, is warm and inviting, while the hinges on the lid are holding up. Inside, heavy silver pieces rest on threadbare blue velvet. The butter knives are held separately in the lid. Small stacks of eight pieces of the rest of the service nestle below. The monogram of the *D* is uneven, showing better on some of the pieces. These are the things that make up my family's archive. Once upon a more spartan time, this silver set – which is still complete and only moderately tarnished – would have been a prized family possession. This silverware was seldom used in the dinners that I ate at the farm. Yet, owned since my grandparents' wedding in the 1940s, at which it was given as a gift, its lustre is somewhat faded. The well-weighted cutlery glimmers alongside a world of readily available, cheap silverware made of semi-disposable grades of steel. The prized possession, the eight carefully kept and tended pieces of each aspect of this service, is languishing. Yet the hope that it represented at that time for a good life, one that was alive with laughter and cheer – and labour, grit and good works – remains, if faintly, in the ways in which I might now choose to honour it.

⸙

Granny did not have much. She grew up in Edmonton, married my grandfather and moved to farms farther north. They leased land at first, then eventually bought a farm with the support of the bank. Grandpa came from a poor family in Manitoba. His father had worked as a farmhand. Granny believed that the things that one did own, even if few in number, should be of quality. Their kitchen table and chairs – the ones currently in our home office – are well made, solid, ornate, yet utterly functional. The everyday dishes, which we use daily, are high-quality stoneware from Norway. The silverware, naturally, complemented the rest. These were things that my grandparents could ill afford, but they were, at the same time, important items. Poverty chipped away at the farm. Bit by bit, the farm was progressively cut into smaller and smaller parcels until little remained. Now it has been sold to another family to struggle through another generation.

{

The silver remains as a quiet, shining emblem of the hope that they had when starting out. Its optimism glows from another era, with its own cruelties and triumphs. It was a hope that did not fail, but that has persisted down the years and into the room in which I write, not far from the kitchen in which my grandparents' silver- and stone-ware resides.

{

It's worth sharing the silver of good times, even though human memory may make the tarnish of hard times easier to remember. I think of the collies, border collies and German shepherds on my grandparents' farm. They were always running through the yard, barking at trucks and keeping coyotes at bay. Cold, northern snows; Boxing Day on the farm; the chill of days spent indoors; the dogs heaped up together in their doghouse, straw-lined for warmth, ice in their shaggy, unbrushed coats. And then the pie, served on the farm plates, stewed beef, roast turkey, potatoes, turnips, Brussels sprouts. Playing with my cousins in the cold basement, the limited selection of games. The wood stove in the corner crackling, mumbling contentedly to itself, heating the room as best it could. Upstairs: adults; the warmth of conversation, coffee and cards; hot air rising. In the yard, the herds. Cattle huddled together, no chickens in the winter – hatched in the spring, butchered in late summer – and the dwindling sheep. The sheep never did make much money for my grandparents – if any at all. I remember once driving the sheared wool to the buyer with Granny. Even though the border collie loved herding them, their coyote-picked numbers dwindled and they all died in the end, as did the geese that swam in the old kiddie pool. All of these things come to me, instant associations with the touch of a soup spoon.

≀

There was, in the end, one goose and one sheep – both old, ornery and near blind – who found a way to get along with one another. The goose perched on the sheep's back, making a nest in her wool. My last memory of both is of them resting like that inside the old barn, breath steaming in the cold, the barn leaning at an improbable angle.

≀

The farms were places of unlikely gathering. There seemed to be little choice but to find ways to get along. There were the Cree and Métis communities, alongside Ukrainians, Poles, French, Anglo-Saxons, Black settlers, Hutterites, all of them figuring out their lives. There were no simple answers. Not everyone got along. Racism abounded, as it does everywhere. Yet there remained points of contact. One could ill afford for there not to be, after all. Sometimes the alternative was to freeze. The sheep and the goose huddled together for warmth. Others did too. The stories of poverty and deprivation, though, still shock me.

⁊

At a writers' festival not long before the pandemic, I was in Edmonton, speaking to a woman who had moved to that city from Toronto. We fell to talking about the communities who ended up in northern Alberta – families like mine, like the Rygas. She said that she wouldn't have expected the mix, the complexity. She was younger, well-read, politically engaged and whip smart.

⁊

The contradictions abound. There are many people who might fit the clichés, but the more we retell those clichés about rural Alberta, the more they risk becoming the only story. We need to tell more, different stories so that we can create more, different futures. My grandparents held meetings around their kitchen table. They were beginning to plan for the farm's organic transition. This would have been in the late 1980s or early 1990s. I recall being there during a meeting with a half-dozen or so other farmers from the area who were also interested. It was not too many years before Granny fell ill and passed away, and the farm was later sold. Yet they did try – they had the will. The contradictions keep piling up: the money to support the land and this organic shift came from my grandfather's trips to the far north in the winters to conduct those seismic explorations. Oil money, then, fed their attempt to become good, organic stewards of the land. Oil on the one hand, environment on the other. Or sometimes both at once.

⁊

It is important that the story doesn't become simpler over time, that the richness is not lost. Here is another part of the complexity: in the 1980s, Granny taught not too far from the farm on a Hutterite colony, before she took up her job in town. Hutterites are a small Anabaptist sect. Granny became a teacher at the age of fifty, after she raised her sons. This was her new, professional role. Her teaching on the colony was not only a background to family life. It also became the subject of her master's degree, which she defended at the University of Alberta two years before she passed away. A copy of her thesis sat unread on my shelves for many years. Titled "Learning from Each Other: The English Teacher on a Hutterite Colony," it documents the ways in which cross-cultural intersections happen with great force and regularity in northern Alberta. It is a place where unlikely neighbours collaborate in order to ensure one another's survival in often unforgiving conditions. The climate, the place, is beautiful – but demanding.

⟨

Granny's thesis is also a document of sound. From the honking of the geese that she and a neighbour purchased from the colony and drove to the farm in the back of her Toyota, to the quiet that she receives from the community when she commits a social misstep and is temporarily shunned, sound permeates her writing. The colony is remote from the other Hutterite colonies in Alberta. It is largely closed off to the world. It is isolated by the Hutterites' German language, religious beliefs and conscious choices. They are also, in Granny's documentation, communal, supportive of one another, kind, at times gregarious and driven to labour in difficult circumstances. What comes through with clarity throughout the thesis is the sound of the water on nearby Baptiste Lake, the sound of the livestock, the language, the meals conducted in silence, the quiet support and the rustle of the crops in the wind.

⟨

As I was reading Granny's thesis, an old photograph fell from the pages. This is the kind of claim that I tend to doubt in others' writing. Yet here it was, happening. What fell from the thesis was a photo of my grandparents much as I remember them: aging farmers. My heavy-set grandfather, hair thinning, has his arm around my granny with her shock of white hair, wearing a skirt and the pair of Birkenstock sandals that she bought when she travelled to Europe with my family around that same time – her first and only trip overseas. I ended up with those sandals. I still wear them around the yard. In the photo, Granny and Grandpa stand next to the picnic table in front of the new farmhouse that they built in the 1980s, the farmhouse that was blessed with indoor plumbing and running water from the well. To my bemusement, Granny writes in her thesis of her surprise that the Hutterites only prioritized building such amenities in their own housing in the late 1970s. Under the deck, on the porch, are pictured two people whom I do not recognize – perhaps because they are too far from the camera. They sit in conversation. The steps alongside the house are visible, as is the dusty dirt next to the house in which I was fond of playing.

ξ

When the picture fell from her thesis with a gentle flapping sound, I realized that it had most likely been put there by Granny herself, nearly thirty years ago. It would have sat there, undisturbed, since that time. The words that she put on these pages, too, sat undisturbed until I was ready for them. I suppose that this is true for all of the words that we put on the page: they lie there, in readiness, for whenever they are received. I know this from visiting some of the world's great libraries, like the Bodleian, Trinity College library in Dublin, the British Library; or some of my personal favourites like the ancient library at the University of Salamanca or the brutalist hub of Robarts Library at the University of Toronto – the last of these being a place in which I have spent a great deal of time. Libraries themselves often do not know what they contain. Millions of words lie in wait for the right reader. Perhaps that reader will arrive – but perhaps the reader won't. From the writer's perspective, it is much the same: we write in the hopes that a reader might arrive. And that is enough. It has to be. In the case of Granny's thesis and the photo lying in wait, whether or not I was the right reader, I did, at length, arrive.

≀

Alongside my love of dumps is my love of cemeteries, and this is where I can visit my grandparents now. In this love I am perhaps less unusual. People write guidebooks to cemeteries. I read often of people who share such an interest. I tour cemeteries when I visit cities, places like Père-Lachaise in Paris, Poets' Corner in Westminster Abbey and Highgate Cemetery in London or the lonely burial site of Anne Brontë in Scarborough, England. These are all places that I remember well. I love small, quiet resting places in the countryside, or urban refuges like Schönhauser Allee Cemetery, the memorial Jewish cemetery in the middle of Berlin. So it is little surprise to me that I am keen on the cemeteries in which my relatives lie. There are two such cemeteries: the South Athabasca Cemetery and the Athabasca Cemetery. The first is a small countryside place of interment, while the second is a larger one on the edge of town.

≀

My relatives on my father's side are buried in the South Athabasca Cemetery. This small plot of land surrounds a disused rural church. It is a modest, white country church, with steeple, pews and altar. There couldn't be more than perhaps a hundred souls buried there, my grandparents among them. The grasses grow long and pick-ups pass by, spitting up gravel. In the nearby fields, the cattle low. Wheat fields make the sounds of wheat fields. I like this graveyard for its simplicity. My grandparents' graves are simple. The church is simple. The trees planted as windbreaks are simple. It is also a humble and humorous cemetery. My favourite tombstone is that of a man with the surname Miller. His headstone has a picture of a semi-trailer on it. The semi-trailer reads, on the side, "It's Miller Time!" I imagine that he must have been a trucker. Then I imagine the oddity of inscribing a now dated beer commercial slogan on one's tombstone. The other stones are perhaps more what one would expect, but the insouciance of Miller's grave sticks with me and sets a more lighthearted tone. The graveyard is peaceful and seldom visited, giving me space for my thoughts when I visit Granny's and Grandpa's graves.

⟩

The main graveyard in Athabasca is more complicated. It is a verita-ble community of the deceased. Situated above the river valley, near the new section of town, it is a good-sized place, covering several acres of trees – aspens and spruces – and lawns. It tells the story of the town, from the uneven, pitching ground at the back in which the child victims of the 1950s polio epidemic lie, to the simple white crosses of the poor, to the orderly rows of stones in the front section. My maternal family's plots are in this graveyard in mixed locations. My great-grandfather is buried farther back, in the uneven terrain that holds many of the older graves. His wife had to be put to rest a few plots away. When she passed away at ninety-two years of age – having just achieved her final goal of outliving the sister with whom she had competed throughout her life – the family discovered that the cemetery had accidentally buried someone else in the plot that had been reserved next to her husband. My aunt is buried in the front section, not far from where her father, my grandfather, lies. Her grave is modest and appropriate. My grandfather's is a two-for-one: my grandmother bought two plots at the same time. A single concrete slab covers both. When she passes, this is where she will lie in anticipation of Judgment.

{

We took Grandma there to visit a few years ago. It was Labour Day weekend, before the pandemic. We had all driven up together, picking her up in Edmonton, where she now lives in order to receive more support. The day was warm and sunny. A light breeze rustled the grasses and turned the leaves on the aspens. We toured the grounds. Grandma paid visits to people whom she had known. We stopped and remarked over interesting graves. There was one that was a copper bust of an old cowboy. Others had logos of the deceased's favourite sports teams. The Saskatchewan Roughriders made multiple appearances. Their fans are loyal even in death. After a while, Grandma steered us toward her husband's grave. Here she paused for a recitation of the Lord's Prayer. Then she mentioned that she had not only bought her own grave, but also the surrounding five, just in case we needed them. What to make of that? I listened to the air moving, to a far-off cow and to a tractor a few fields over. An awkward pause followed Grandma's announcement. One of the children interrupted it with the blessedly helpful irreverence of the young. The graves, silent, seemed to smile at our human predicaments.

{

How do I represent the people around whom I have lived? How about those who live on the land about which I write? I cannot write about the land, the north of Alberta, without touching the people who live there – those whom I know, and those whom I do not know. I have to make a series of decisions. I am responsible for what I put on the page, and words have power. There are some solutions that I reject. Not to write, for instance, would be to ignore the story and the history – or at least not to share it for what good it may do. I seriously consider this option, far more seriously than these words on the page might suggest. It takes me decades of experience and thinking to get to the point where I can write these words. Even still, I feel their limitations. Yet I move on, hoping and trusting that others will add to what I am able to record.

{

To tell these stories, but to tell them without any of the difficult bits, or only to make everyone look good, is also not the right approach. While we may be good at polishing the glass of time, leaving the dirty bits out when telling our lives to our children, that option, too, is false. I can't stick just to the happy stories. The happy ending might be nice in principle, and it celebrates everyone who struggled to live to the best of their ability – but it erases what those struggles were – and they were real. Yet to revel in the most sordid details is also not right for me. Many stories are not mine to tell. Many stories, even the truest ones, have the power to wound, and so must be told only with purpose and clarity. Writing is a fast-flowing current, sweeping the writer along when it goes well, but with many murky eddies like the flats at Athabasca Landing, and with many a rock against which one might be dashed in the rapids.

{

To tell how my paternal grandfather ended his life with good deeds, for instance, it is first necessary to understand some of his faults.

The good that he was able to do for others through Alcoholics Anonymous – about which my family only learned the depths at his funeral – was only possible because he was an alcoholic. So while I remain committed to the principle that one should avoid speaking ill of the dead, we must speak of the complex soil of life in which we spread our roots in order to speak well of the dead, too. How do I relate to you what my grandfather was to me? One cannot write without upsetting some readers, but neither is it necessary to set out deliberately to offend. My writing might irritate or anger some of my family, so I consult with other writers to see how they handle the issue. One never speaks to their family at all. Another doesn't speak to them about the writing. Another sends the work to them only when it is published. "Never read my lines," I once read in a poem by George Bowering addressed to his daughter. But of course she did just that – people will. I offer some family members the chance to read – but not censor – pieces of my work before going forward. They are important readers to honour. Other readers are largely imaginary. I settle on a path forward: to tell the stories as they exist for me. I think of my grandfather: gruff, quiet, removed. He napped every day after lunch. Every evening, after a long day in the fields, he and Granny watched the news on the CBC before going to bed. I associate him with the sounds of creaking hips, wrenches clanging on cold concrete floors, muttered curses. He was forever in the fields or in the garage, as far as I could tell. As he grew quite deaf as he aged, it became clear that a lifetime of hard listening wore out his ability to hear. This is not the same grandfather he was to others, nor the father who he was earlier in this life, nor the husband who was often away up north.

⁂

Even so, the problems of representation do not subside. Instead of fabricating characters and situations that lead to sticky politics, I can claim some refuge in the reality that underlies the situation. I cannot tell the story without invoking the people who live in northern Alberta. In fiction, the circumstances might differ. Instead, another worry: that of misrepresenting the real people or actual events. Writing about real people makes them unreal, changes them. Words are deeply imperfect tools, too – stand-ins for ideas, experiences, events and things, always existing at a remove from those things in themselves.

‹

What can I say about Jewish identities and anti-Semitism among the people who have long lived in northern Alberta? It may seem like a jump, but it demonstrates some of the challenges. One of the seemingly obscure northerly figures about whom I heard, from north of the bridge, was a Jewish man known locally just as Yaggi. Yaggi was of my grandparents' generation, a trader who would arrive at intervals at the family's remote farm, selling the sorts of goods that could only be bought in town when the roads were passable and the river traversable. He was described to me – although how much of this memory is by now my own confabulation I do not know – as driving a horse and carriage, the latter of which unfolded into a moving shop. That carriage-shop displayed brushes, knives, stockings, pudding mix and other non-perishable goods that the farms would run out of during their wintry isolation. I never learned his surname, nor much more about him except that he came sometimes and that everyone in Richmond Park and the neighbouring district of Big Coulee – where one set of my great-grandparents ran the country store and gas station – knew him. Many of the farmers in the area were Eastern European in origin, none too far from their homelands in spirit if not in body. I have long wondered about how many of those families might themselves have been Jewish, or former

Jews, leaving persecution, surnames and religion behind when they arrived in Canada. It could even be possible that the Rabins in my own family did so, given their name, though I have no evidence. They pronounced it *Rah-bin*, not *Rah-been*. My great-grandmother on that side was also, I was told, anti-Semitic. But the lone and apparently lonely figure of Yaggi sticks out in my mind, stereotypes clinging to the sides of his cart as he tinkered from one farm to the next.

𝄽

My work has trained me to question origins. It has trained me to listen for the story behind the story. Any origin leads back to further points, genealogies spinning off in myriad directions. Any beginning comes from somewhere. In historical terms, origins might just be the point at which the records taper off. I search my family's stories and records with a knowledge that the tapering off is part of the tracery of time.

𝄽

What I think I know: my maternal grandfather's side of the family came to Turtle Island from areas of Silesia that are today split between Poland and the Czech Republic. Cieszyn, where the Rabins came from, is a couple of villages away from what later became Auschwitz, near the Polish-Czech border. The other side of the family, the Goras, came from farther south, in what is today part of the Czech Republic. They arrived in North America and then made their way west and north, eventually settling in Richmond Park.

𝄽

The family left Silesia in the late nineteenth and early twentieth centuries, before the First World War. It was a time of displacements in central and Eastern Europe. Poverty, conflict, pogroms, bloodshed and more drove people to seek new beginnings. The government of Canada promised a better life for European emigrants after the Canadian Pacific Railway was completed and Louis Riel was executed, linked events that took place only a few days apart in late 1885. What can be said for those immigrants, the Goras and the Rabins? The records are fairly sparse. Eastern Europe is incredibly complex.

⁊

When, for instance, I search the records of the Shoah, which took place in that immediate environment, I find many Goras and many Rabins. There are many who died at Auschwitz. Were these people relatives who were left behind in Europe? I have no immediate reason to think so. Both names are common. Populations in Eastern Europe were repeatedly displaced. And those who died at Auschwitz arrived there for a range of reasons: although most were Jewish prisoners, some were political dissenters, queer folks and more. Those who fell outside of the Nazi vision, those who resisted the Nazi occupation.

⁊

Auschwitz feels impossibly fraught because of the historical record, the mass trauma and the death that lingers in the air. I am surprised that my endeavours to listen to the landscapes of northern Alberta point me to such a place. It feels both very distant and yet close. My family's tenuous historical connections to that region, coming from a nearby village, are recorded in a single instance. It took me well over a year to be able to start to try writing about travelling there. I made myself work through that experience as the seventy-fifth anniversary of the liberation of Auschwitz arrived. Try as I might, the words failed to come together. It is important to honour the place, yet I think of all of the other accounts of the Holocaust that are more eloquent and more deeply informed than mine ever could be. *The Diary of a Young Girl* by Anne Frank, the works of Primo Levi, *Maus* by Art Spiegelman, films like *Life Is Beautiful*. It took a global pandemic to wrest the words out of me, and even still I pause.

≀

We travelled to Auschwitz in 2017 when, at length, I was finally able to visit this particular country of my family's origins. We started by getting on a small tour bus in Kraków. The bus drove for about forty-five minutes through a Polish countryside of small farms, ruins and closed factories. As we drove, we watched a documentary on small, scratchy screens. The documentary was about the liberation of Auschwitz. It was terrible to watch and contrasted markedly with the spring landscape that we saw out the windows. At length, our bus became one of the many that pulled up to the site. The weather was grey and cloudy. Later it rained. People piled off the buses. There was a small cafeteria, a bookshop and washrooms. It felt austere, while also attempting to welcome travellers somewhat as other tourist destinations might. It was located off a minor road in the Polish countryside and could easily be driven past if one did not know the enormity of what transpired in this place.

≀

The tour of Auschwitz has remained basically unchanged since the 1950s, for many good and not so good reasons. Yet what struck me most about touring the place in the early twenty-first century was the reality of mobile phones. I have an on-again, off-again relationship with such devices. I question the value of constant connectivity, even as more and more people have them. At Auschwitz, what mobile devices enabled was the taking of pictures. There were phones clicking all over the place as we entered, passing first through security, then through the infamous "Arbeit Macht Frei" sign atop Auschwitz's main gate. What, my partner and I wondered, could it be like to be the person in charge of mending and replacing that weathered sign? Then we saw people taking selfies under the sign. What, I found myself wondering with greater urgency, would one do with a selfie taken under that sign? I recoiled, unsure but upset.

꙳

You tour Auschwitz in groups organized according to language, and so we began a tour in English, in and out of the buildings that were used for bunking prisoners. Displays told the story of the documentary evidence, seeming to anticipate rebukes or denial. We walked, feet heavy on the stairwells, shoes crunching on gravel walkways between buildings. We were quiet as our guide led us with efficiency and tact. We were given enough space to take in the scale and scope of Auschwitz – encapsulated perhaps best in the ordinary brick nature of the drab buildings – but not enough time to truly break down in a manner that would befit the place. Yet the trip became more complicated as we continued. There are a few rooms where one is asked not to take photographs. Out of a similar spirit of respect for the dead, I will forgo describing those rooms. They defy representation. Those who have been there will know what I mean. In those rooms, as we toured in stunned silence, I heard a clicking. Visitors had their phones out and were taking photos. Those with traditional cameras appeared to have followed the clear message of the signage – images of crossed-out cameras, pictographs comprehensible across language divides – but some mobile phone users were snapping pictures. I wanted to snap their phones in half. "Don't," my partner said. Let the ill of it be on their own heads, she implied. Yet perhaps I might say something gentle-yet-firm, just to the young, twenty-ish woman who was the worst offender, clearly attempting to hide her snaps from view? "Don't," my partner said again, distressed now not only by what we were witnessing, but also by the casual displays of horrendous disrespect – and also by my anger. I didn't. But I kept listening. The tour went on, past the wall used for executions, and then through the smaller incinerators that were used for burning the bodies of the murdered. Of this room I remembered images from my education. These images stood out like the film footage of corpses pushed into mass graves by bulldozers, footage that I had just seen anew in the film we had watched during the drive. What was striking was how small the room was. It was an underground bunker that you could easily miss. This part of the tour then brought us back to the gates, to the canteen, bookshop and washrooms, and then to the bus for the second, much larger part of the day.

𝄽

Auschwitz is not one site, but multiple sites. The two main sites, and the two that are part of the public tours, are Auschwitz and Auschwitz-Birkenau. Birkenau was built later and is much, much larger than Auschwitz. It was grey and rainy by the time that we arrived and entered via the gate through which the trains also once arrived. In contrast to Auschwitz, Birkenau is more poorly preserved. Much of the woodwork, including many bunkhouses, is in ruins. The brick-sided rows of the remaining bunkhouses stretched far away in every direction as our group walked, walked and walked, our guide showing us elements of the documentary evidence to tie this place to the events that happened there late in the war. At length, we arrived at what had been the two main crematoria, destroyed by retreating Nazi troops. Two disordered piles of bricks and concrete slabs were explained by our guide and by nearby plaques. A large memorial to the victims of the Shoah stood nearby, with writing in many languages. It occupied our attention for quite some time, as did the pits around the blasted furnaces.

꙳

It was here that we noticed very little grows – or was growing that day – at Birkenau. There was a ring of stunted trees near the crematorium site. These seemed sickly. Ground cover was perhaps beginning to reclaim the bunkhouses, but their rectangular shapes stood out clearly. We visited one bunkhouse that was still standing and that had been decorated by child prisoners. Then we visited a privy where some plants pushed up. However, relatively little was growing. None of it seemed to be thriving. What does the land remember? We paused, listened. Beyond the gates, trees waved in a rainy springtime dance. There were birds in those trees, life beyond the camp. Inside, though, the trees appeared stunted or dead. It was eerie. Visitors' voices carried, as did their slow footsteps on gravel. The land seemed to ask us to listen.

꙳

There is a more overt link to Canada at Auschwitz than those that I might find in any of the fragmentary archives of my family's Polish provenance. One part of Auschwitz was used as a holding space, a depository, for the goods brought to the camp by the prisoners. It was where the goods resided, and sometimes prisoners were sent there. The incarcerated called it "going to Canada," apparently because they equated Canada with the land of plenty. Knowing only too well my country's historical mistreatment of Jewish people during the war – their resettlement refused, the slogan "none is too many" floating on the racist under- and over-currents – this moniker came as a shock to me. Canada can indeed be a land of plenty

– but for whom? Under what circumstances? And at what costs? I am, as you would expect, not the first one to remark on the camp's expression of "going to Canada." After our visit, I find a reflection on Auschwitz written by Métis writer Warren Cariou. He writes – movingly, compellingly – of his own parallel discovery, in a manner that I expect anyone coming to Auschwitz from Canada might, with a mix of shock and defamiliarization.

≀

When we left Birkenau, we also parted with our tour group. They were returning to Kraków, but we needed to get to Sosnowiec, a city not too far away. We asked to be dropped in Oświęcim, the town that houses Auschwitz on its outskirts. We disembarked at the station and managed to get tickets for the train. A food vendor sold us roast chicken and buns. We ate on the platform, hungered by the emotional drain of the day and from our grim fast while in the camp. The train station was empty aside from a few other travellers. Weeds grew in the tracks. The signage, in Polish and English, was graffitied. The architecture was heavy on concrete. The weather continued to be grey, the clouds low, a chill breeze blowing. It was desolate. At length, our train pulled up. It was a no-nonsense commuter train, even more heavily graffitied than the station. One had to pick seats with care in order to find a window that was not covered by paint. The on-board toilet was dire. The train then departed, trundling us slowly, loudly along the countryside. There were small farms, shanty settlements along railroad easements, towns, villages and former factories sliding into rural ruin. Five hundred years ago, it might have been castles and villages falling apart. In our time it's cinder-block factories.

≀

Derelict spaces fascinate me. What becomes derelict? What do we preserve and what do we shed? There is as much, if not more, to learn from derelict spaces as there is to gather from carefully preserved ones. I think of the grain elevators of the Prairies. The ones in Athabasca were taken down during my childhood, after many years of quiet decrepitude. The tracks that led there have long been disused, yet still cross the road downtown. I think of the farm, the old barn collapsing into the ground in slow motion. Or I think of the old one-bedroom farmhouse, abandoned for years before its demolition, and of the large frog in the basement that stared up at me one time when I snuck in and chanced the rickety stairs.

⸙

The day had been exhausting. It was not over yet, though. Looking at the Polish countryside, we saw neo-Nazi graffiti. Swastikas popped up a few times, as well as slogans in English that I needn't repeat. We were aghast. What could explain this horrible repetition of hatred and xenophobia? So close to Auschwitz, yet so far. Poland was clearly broke, at least in this region. Formerly productive places lay fallow. The standard of living appeared to be poor. Were these not similar to some of the conditions that were linked to the rise of anti-Semitism in Nazi Germany? For all of the time since the Holocaust, and for all of the learning, how can today still make the mistakes of yesterday?

⸙

At length, the train deposited us in Katowice, a transfer on the way to our next destination. The station was attached to a mall, an emblem of the new shiny glass architecture of the European Union. The gap between what we saw in the countryside and in the shopping centre was disarming. We arrived late to our hotel and fell into bed, too tired to process meaning.

⸮

That night, I dreamt that I was in a different bed, one in which I hadn't slept in at least twenty years. Perhaps it was because both beds sagged, pushing my body toward the middle. Perhaps it was the shared smell of the rooms. Perhaps it was because the other bed, the bed that I slept in at Grandma's house, in the chill basement, held for me myriad reminiscences of Eastern Europe. Half-turning, half-asleep, I recalled Grandma's basement. After her husband died and she sold the farm, the home in town became her residence for decades. It was a house that I loved – and that I also, as a young, shy child, viewed with some trepidation. The basement had a bedroom, tucked into the corner, in which my parents slept when we visited. My sister and I slept in the basement family room. The room held two single beds, formerly bunk beds from the farm, but by then separated and laid out on different walls. There was a sofa that was most often unusable beneath a sea of flotsam. The basement was a mix of remembrances, from a trunk full of my deceased aunt's clothing, to grainy black-and-white pictures of my grandfather and his Polish relatives, to boxes of extra dishes and Lord knows what else. In the next room, the cold room, pickles and preserves wafted their invitations. I recalled the sleepy feeling of watching the space heater that Grandma brought out when we visited. I watched its glowing element and heard its electric hum as I drifted off. I worried that its heat might ignite the board on which Grandma placed the heater so that it would not scorch the pile of the shag carpet. In the mornings, the heater would be off, unplugged by one of the adults in the night. The board was darkened by the rickety heater. I would lay there in the mornings, embraced by the tight hug of the sagging mattress. One by one, my fingers would emerge. I would touch the plywood panel of the wall next to the bed, sensing the cold. The chill hardened the varnish and separated that coating from the wood. I listened to the peeling and chipping sound as I woke myself up by helping the varnish along. The senses and memory – beds, like tables, transported me elsewhere, to other times, other sounds than the low whine of traffic on the Polish streets below.

≀

I was beginning to be able, finally, to write about the experience of being in Poland as the seventy-fifth anniversary of the liberation of Auschwitz neared. And then our cat died after a short, unpleasant pancreatic illness. I will always claim that my rural roots make me tough when it comes to pets. In northern Alberta, cats and dogs were taken out behind the proverbial shed when they fell ill. But of course I wept for the cat. I wept, too, looking over photographs of the cat that charted my children growing into themselves, a feline presence always there to console or accompany them through life's changes. She had been our second cat – though of course there is no meaningful sense in which we possessed her, except that she was among the animals who formed our collective. Our male orange tabby cat, who came a year before her, had died a few years earlier. I miss them both, if not all of their smells, messes and habits. Our tabby liked to eat anything with string or tassels. The house remains tassel-free as a result.

≀

Both of our cats lived longer, though, than did my first childhood cat. He was a stray adopted by my parents when they were university students. He lived with us until I was five. He was a disagreeable, sharp-clawed orange feline. My only memories of him are

1. being clawed by him;

2. being clawed by him that other time, the time the log jumped out of the fire; and

3. watching him barf all over the sidewalk in front of the bungalow that we rented for one year near Queen Elizabeth Park in Vancouver in the early 1980s.

Of course, I loved him nonetheless.

⁂

Our cat left us after my sister was born. She was – and is – allergic to cats. But allergies were less well understood then, so that was viewed in part as just an inconvenience. The eventual and final reason that our family gave him up was that he brought home fleas, which I then caught. So the cat went to live on Granny and Grandpa's farm. To my young mind, that sounded fair enough. I would be free of fleas, while our cat would be free to romp the four quarter sections of trees, fields, barns, gardens – with cows, sheep, dogs, geese, chickens and other cats for company. He didn't last long, however. I don't remember when I heard the news, but he disappeared from the farm not too long after arriving.

⁂

A few years later, Granny was out walking, as she always was. As she went, she cleared downed trees from the fences, checked on the progress of the crops and visited the cattle. The dogs went with her, running along in the forests and across the fields. On this particular walk, she found a feline skull. It could have been a skunk, or it could have been a cat – the two are similar. I never fully learned which it was for certain. The skull had been picked clean and was weather-bleached to a bright white. It was therefore unlike many of the carcasses that I had inspected out on the back quarter. That was where Grandpa took dead cattle and sheep to be picked apart by the coyotes. Those skulls that I had kicked over had had fascinating colonies of maggots squirming inside of them, writhing little worms picking away the flesh as they incubated themselves. Instead, this skull came back clean.

⸘

As was the habit on the farm, Granny placed the skull on the shelf in the downstairs living room. This shelf was reserved for such things. I loved the shelf. It held a bird's skull, as well as a cleaned cow's skull. There was an assortment of deer antlers that had been found in the woods, as well as cow horns and hooves that had been shed. The most vibrant feathers from migrating birds ended up there too. And now this skull. I believed that it had belonged to my long-lost cat, though I couldn't prove it either way. Yet it's a belief onto which I hold. Doing so suits me and provides me with an end to my cat's story. I lamented the loss of my cat throughout my childhood and early adulthood. Our later cats served as substitutes for the lost innocence that came with my first cat's death. It was the first death that I knew in a way that was meaningful for me. I was, in a sense, happy with the skull's being on the basement shelf. I looked at it often, contemplating its small size, its fragility, the large sockets for eyes and the array of fine, sharp teeth. It was an early memento mori. The land helps us to process such losses, first by processing them back into the earth, and second by reminding us of new life to come in each season's cycle.

⸘

The cats in my life – as well as the dogs – remind me, again and again, of the limitations that hamper my own thinking. They show me a part of what it might mean to listen better to the land. They help by pointing out the ways in which I have too often limited my listening to the act of listening to people. I realize these limits well when I read French thinker Jacques Derrida's encounter with his cat in an essay that is well-known in academic circles. I've grown fond of Derrida, not just as a thinker who never quite fit the label of continental philosophy under which his work is studied, but also as a flawed intellectual, scribbling away in his too-small attic piled with books just outside of Paris. The essay shows the sort of quirky humility that might be necessary in order to listen to the world. So I want to follow his thinking and see where I, too, hit my limits.

⁊

Derrida starts by wishing that the words that he uses when he writes could be, in themselves, "naked." The nudity that he talks about is more like transparency, a wish that words could convey what they intend to mean. Yet the relationship between the word and the idea or thing is never simple. This wish for "naked" words is never possible in language. This is a challenge that has been debated for thousands of years, at least since Plato. Meaning lies trapped behind the veils of words, and so we find ourselves bumbling along. It's with this nudity in mind that Derrida encounters his cat. It is an unusual and unlikely moment in his writing. It's a personal touch – and it seems like a comparatively transparent (or naked) one. The cat, Derrida suggests, can see him naked. The cat can see his nudity for what it is. That nakedness takes away all of the fancy parts of being human. It leaves behind an animal. Here is how he writes of it: "I often ask myself, just to see, *who I am* – and who I am (following) at the moment when, caught naked, in silence, by the gaze of an animal, for example the eyes of a cat, I have trouble, yes, a bad time overcoming my embarrassment." I love the image that this passage conjures up. Here is an aging Derrida, maybe already carrying the cancer that would lead to his death in a few years, with his shock of white hair, nude in front of his cat. Perhaps it is the morning and he is in the bedroom. Or maybe he is in the kitchen sneaking a midnight snack. It is a touching image, an honest one full of sympathy for a thinker who, after all, was just another fleshy being, standing there, naked and embarrassed, in front of his cat.

≀

The problem is that the cat, as Derrida writes of her, seems somehow to be simpler than he himself is. He goes on from this moment of nudity to diagnose his shame over his body, and then moves on to the problem of feeling shame in general. As a result, he manages to circle back to human concerns, making them more important than those of his cat – just at the moment when he seems to strip away the differences. But a passage late in the essay makes me think again. Derrida is considering the history of philosophy, and he specifically considers male philosophers like René Descartes, Immanuel Kant, Martin Heidegger, Jacques Lacan and Emmanuel Levinas. He says the following about them: "Their discourses are sound and profound, but everything goes on as if they themselves had never been looked at, and especially not naked, by an animal that addressed them." What does it mean to be looked at, naked, by an animal that addresses us? What does it mean to be listened to, naked, by an animal that calls to us? How does that gaze or listening impact our thinking, especially if the cat that looks and listens to our naked bodies does not bring us back to our shame, but instead reminds us of how little we can possibly know? What is the cat herself thinking?

≀

When our ("our"!) cat was dying, she indeed looked at each of us to address us. She spoke to us softly, meowing a seeming request. I think that she addressed us in order to let us know she had decided that it was time for her to go, some dozen plus years since we had brought her stray self into our home. Because we were not yet ready, we were at first unable to meet her look – this cat who had seen us all naked at one time or another – and so we tried veterinary interventions that were beyond what she was willing to bear. After that happened, she stopped meeting our gaze until we stopped and let events take their course. She seemed ashamed of us, averting her clouding eyes until we acquiesced and helped her on her final journey.

⁊

How, I wonder, can we meet the cat's address when it shows us not our difference, but instead our inadequacy? What does it mean, what could it mean, to cease placing human concerns at the centre of our attention?

III

It is the trees – uncanny, possessed of depths and mystery, and feral in ways beyond my ken – which take priority over any terminology.
– Matthew Battles, *Tree*

For the ear, the most vital thing that can be listened to here is silence. To bend the ear to silence is to discover how seldom it is there. Always something moves. . . . But now and then come an hour when the silence is all but absolute, and listening to it one slips out of time.
– Nan Shepherd, *The Living Mountain*

Tables, as people tend to think of them, are made from trees. They are trees, transformed into the flat surfaces on which humans perform their daily rituals. They are hard yet also forgiving. They record the bumps of dropped dishes, the nicks of wayward cutlery and the scrapings of crafts. In itself, a "table continues to be wood, an ordinary, sensuous thing," as Karl Marx puts it in an often-discussed passage from his magnum opus, *Capital*. But tables, such as our dining-room table, become more complicated items. We can also sell and buy tables, and this is where Marx's interest lies, because then a table "transcends sensuousness" and becomes part of the market. At that point, the table "evolves out of its wooden brain grotesque ideas, far more wonderful than if it were to begin dancing of its own free will." Marx goes on from there to introduce what he calls commodity fetishism. Like so many of Marx's commentators, though, I get hung up on the images. Wooden tables seldom stand on their heads, nor do they tend to break into dance. Yet I can with ease imagine our dining-room table doing either or both of those things. Perhaps at the same time. It rests, firm and cool under the palms of my hands, evoking the sensuous wonder of the forests from whence it came. This sensuous wonder holds within it all of the potential of the table, the potential of song and dance. The table holds the trace, too, of the woodlands to which, more and more, I find myself turning.

≀

Consider the deep roots of the forests. What do trees know? What do they say? To borrow from anthropologist Eduardo Kohn, what do they think? Consider Pando. Perhaps the world's oldest living organism, as well as the heaviest, it looks to human eyes like an aspen forest in the state of Utah. But it is all a single entity, sprung from the same roots. It is now at risk due to human incursions. But listen: A deep fissure and thrust, the voice of water moving through soil. The sifting of roots, rhizomes and fungi, leading the way deeper and out – a meaning held, fingertip to tip, sharing across the biomass of a region. Species speaking to species. The things that are, for humans, unexpected.

≀

We travelled north in autumn to see Granny and to visit the family on what would become one of my last visits to see her. My then girl-friend, who remains one of my best friends, came on the trip as well.

The visit to the hospital was awkward. It was abbreviated and inadequate. I remember the clinical smell, the sterile sound and Granny, shrinking back from the world that had been her home for so long. She was apologetic for the state in which she found herself. She was embarrassed, accustomed as she was to being strong, to being able to carry on in spite of hardship. Maybe it was later that day, or maybe it was the next day, but the only other thing that I remember from that trip is listening to the aspens. My girlfriend and I sat out in the tree house that my father and I had built ten years previous. That tree house stood in the forest behind the farmhouse and was where the coyotes came each night to howl. It was made of old boards that Dad and I had scavenged from the farm. In the corners and joints, butterflies wove their cocoons. My girlfriend and I sat there, just looking out the window. This window faced west, away from the house. I recall watching the forest and hearing the sound of the trees as they bumped up against one another and as their leaves whispered in the wind. To me, it was – and is – the sound of solace.

⁌

Trees are vegetables. Plants. They speak their own dialects. Aspen poplar. Cottonwood. Birch. Willow. Caragana. Alder. Pine, spruce, fir. Douglas, Sitka, white, blue, black, lodgepole, Jack. Larch, tamarack. Cedar: red, yellow, giant. Wood fibre, membranes. Cambium, bark, brown, root. Canopy. The language of trees is as dense as the boreal. The words overlap as do the leaves of the canopy above. Let both stay as dense – we need the language of the trees. The scent of the language is heady with both growth and decay. Sapling, nurse log, runner, taproot. The sound of the language is earthy, redolent, resonant. The growth of leaves, unfurled in the spring sunshine. Stomata. The understorey, the overstorey.

⁌

On the other side there is the language of industry. Deadfall, clutter, entanglement. Snare. Snag. Switches of branches, criss-crossing in a barrier to work.

⁋

Take the lightning-struck core of an ancient cedar. Hear the voice, its damp echo from within. The song that lies at the core, at the heart. Raise into song the soft rot at the heartwood, carbon restored to the soil beneath, the humus on which we are weaned. The source of our common wealth: the logs of our cabins, the papers of our travails, the canoes of our travels. Listen: trees speak. I try to hear the trees and their kin, in part via those who have come before, lighting the path. Listening to the fruitful murmuration of the trees, speaking a soft thrum and whish of a world in turmoil.

⁋

In Henry David Thoreau's *Walden*, there is a well-known chapter called "sounds." It fits wonderfully within the book. Among other things, *Walden* is an exercise in listening. Thoreau's two-year retreat to his hand-built cabin in nineteenth-century Concord, Massachusetts, provides a lovely, boisterous reflection on the toils of daily life and the exhaustion of living in a noisy and brash society. So Thoreau, in his retreat, takes the time to pause and listen. What does he hear? Thoreau hears birdsong, the swaying of trees, the bubbling of the pond nearby, the frogs, the understorey. What a wonderful word that is: *understorey*. In ecological terms, it refers to the intertwined layers of growth on the forest floor, the vegetation that thrives out of direct sunlight. I suppose that it means something like *basement* – the storey that is at the base of all others. But what a story it is. The story of life that exists out of the sunshine, the hushed layer of meaning generated from below, from the warm roots that reach their way into the rotted boughs of trees as they die, fungi running ahead of them. Charlotte Gill, in her memoir of tree planting in British Columbia, *Eating Dirt*, puts it as follows: "Sometimes the only sound, besides the dripping, is the silent roar of matter breaking down and melting back into the soil." These are the sounds of the forest.

⁂

Thoreau noticed from Walden Pond, however, that he still heard the trains running to and from Boston. He noticed the incursions that humans made, just as I notice in my day-to-day life that I always hear traffic. It is a steady hum of petroleum burning, even while I am listening to the gentle *cheese-bur-ger* song that the black-capped chickadees make in late winter from high in the spruces. Even now, with the traffic sounds winter-muted, with the number of vehicles having decreased due to the pandemic, I still struggle to hear the understorey. I notice how little I am immersed in it.

⁂

Listen: listen to snow falling. Its muffling effect on all things. The day is perhaps quietest when it snows. Traffic sounds fall away unless the vehicles are close at hand, crunch-rolling over compacting flakes. Snow. Listen. I am struck by what it can mean to listen to the land. For the Syilx Okanagan writer Jeannette Armstrong, in a piece called "Land Speaking," it is just that: the land speaks. She also asserts that the act of speaking her Indigenous Okanagan language is an act of being one with the land, of speaking the land. Can I, as a settler, find a way to connect with the land? I do not have an answer to that question, though I am mindful of the ways in which xwélméxw theorist Dylan Robinson notes that settlers' positions as listeners differ from those of Indigenous peoples. Robinson suggests the idea of "hungry listening" as a way to consider how settlers listen to Indigenous concepts in order to consume them. While I am aware that I always risk doing so, I hope, in observing Indigenous thinking about listening, that I can share these ideas with you without presenting them as my own. In a 2018 interview, Oji-Cree Indigiqueer writer Joshua Whitehead used the term *fierce listening* in a context that might build on Armstrong's thoughts: the act of fierce listening, Whitehead contends, "is a strategy . . . to learn from our elders, mothers or aunties." Whitehead advocates listening across generations and times, listening to those who might surround one with care. Armstrong's listening to the landscape speaking is comparable – a lesson to which we might listen, even if I cannot join her in the same space. For her, the act of speaking is a form of territorial embodiment. What is the impact, then, of listening to the land, listening to the snow fall – the snow covering the sound itself? The act of listening pairs with the act of speaking. I start by listening to the land. Perhaps that is something that settlers might usefully learn how to do, even if from a distance. Being here, in and of itself, listening, witnessing, in the humming, buzzing environment is perhaps enough.

≀

Out in the bush, a day of snow when the regular sounds of life fade away. A blanketing white that surrounds with sleep. The flakes fall, a branch ruffles in a cascade of light-drawn sparkle. Hexagons flash in the sunshine. What senses does one need? A cracked stick, the crunch of snow over needles underfoot. A nose, lifted. A sound.

≀

What I have written up to this point is a nurse log, ready for new growth. Perhaps this situation is true for everyone who gets to continue to write over time. In the last few years, I wrote a series of academic essays about the concept of being human. I was interested in who wields the label of *human*, as well as those the label can include or exclude. Yet as I bumped up against the edges of language and that troublesome label, *human*, it was only a short step to thinking about how that label also controls, orders and organizes the non-human or the more-than-human worlds. I may struggle to see the environmental relations in which we are held, but I am learning. So even though I can't yet tell the difference between trees just by listening to their branches in the wind, I am starting to learn. I listen in order to let go.

≀

While I was busily listening to humans in the past, ecologists were reporting alarming drops in the populations of birds across North America. Billions of birds lost to deforestation, habitat destruction, pollution, hunting, being smacked into windows, flattened by cars, sucked into jets, eaten by house cats, poisoned, lost, killed, lost, lost. The loss of avian biodiversity is staggering. The world is losing its birdsong alarmingly fast. The music of the world, when it comes to birds, is becoming quieter.

≀

On the southern end of my paternal family's farm stood the Meanook Biological Research Station. It was owned and operated for many years by the University of Alberta. I was told as a child that it was located where it was because it stood in the middle of the province. It turns out that, in terms of latitude, at 54°35' it is very close to the 54°50' that marks the middle of the north-south axis. It is not particularly close, however, in terms of longitude. It is worth noting even to Albertans that the geographical midpoint of the province is in fact a solid hour-and-a-half drive north of Edmonton. Edmonton is usually considered a pretty northerly place, but it is still in the south. That's a bit besides my point, though, you might say. The Meanook observatory, Granny shared with me, was devoted in part to the study of birds. Warblers, jays, sparrows, swallows, hawks, owls and more come through the land. Some birds arrive as passing guests on the wing. Others are long-term residents. Granny knew the warblers and thrushes from their throaty songs.

{

The old farm, when I pass it now, is full of rundown equipment. There are fewer trees. The land is more open, and the ground looks worn down. Soil becomes depleted. The aspens and birches were already making way for a spruce forest back then. I had pulled downed trees off the barbed-wire fences whenever I had walked in the forests. I had listened for the birdsong – before it would be gone. It is a necessary biodiversity. The birds are the metaphorical and literal canaries in our open-air coal mines for seeds, crops, livestock – let alone cities, humans, roads.

{

The Meanook observatory is now called the Meanook National Wildlife Area, and is administered by Environment Canada. *Meanook* is a Cree word that means "a good camping place." It lies just above the Tawatinaw Valley – Cree for "river which divides the hills" – in north-central Alberta. Of late, the old observatory there has been deemed expensive and no longer worth the upkeep. So it has been shuttered. Now the area consists of some fields – ones that my grandfather used to lease for haying – as well as some wetlands and old buildings. For many years, these buildings housed equipment for biological and geological measurement and analysis. These formal functions, however, are no more. Ruins remain as, over the years, scientific interest could not sustain the costs of maintenance. Scientists and graduate students at the station sometimes visited the farm, Granny told me when I was a child. She was proud to have them nearby, monitoring the warblers and nuthatches, making space for the moose and bears. The slough on the south end of the farm, I realize now, must drain toward Meanook. On its southern end, Meanook has a water hole dug in order to provide water to fight forest fires. There are frogs, salamanders, ducks, geese.

}

"We choose the landscapes we live in," writes Hamilton-based writer and carpenter John Terpstra. "Forget or ignore the stories, neglect to enter or hold up your side of the conversation, and all you are left with is what is in front of your eyes. And that will likely be a highly engineered environment made out of concrete." I've been running that risk of late. It's late in the winter by now, the crusted snow has refrozen overnight and I am grumpily wading through another pandemic day that leaves me feeling drained. I am slipping into an engineered environment made of concrete. It is a world that is designed to contain my day-to-day movements, to anticipate those movements, to capitalize upon them. The average day outside of our home feels like the gentle squeeze of a vise as we wait on the news in hushed tones. Inside the home, everyone is weary, nursing colds that could be – but turn out not to be – evidence of the virus.

}

I imagine forward and back, the power of remembrance and story needed to break the frame of the everyday. I think of strawberries, wild strawberries. Not the flavourless husks sold in the grocery store at this time of year, but real strawberries. Potawatomi botanist

Robin Wall Kimmerer describes strawberries as "a gift," one that ties us into a reciprocal relationship with the land. I think of the perfect strawberry, the sound that a strawberry makes. On the farm there was a field in the back quarter where wild strawberries grew. I cannot say that the space was natural, not exactly. It was engineered in that settlers cleared the field, in this case the settlers who had come before my grandparents. They made space for the strawberries to crawl across the open land. Granny taught me much of what I learned as a child about wild plants, including strawberries. I often think of them as a June berry, an early fruit crop, but that month is the beginning for the domesticated varieties. The wild ones are better and come later. The delicate, white, five-petalled flowers give way to small, green nubs of fruit that then grow and ripen, passing from white to red. Uneaten berries fall to the ground and germinate their seeds, or else are consumed – favoured as they are by many species, from humans to bears and beyond – and then they are transported by gut to new destinations. Strawberries also reproduce by sending out runners – small, red shoots that push in all directions and take root in adjacent soils.

⁊

It was likely that latter method of reproduction – the spreading threads of strawberry shoots – that led to much of that patch in the pasture on the farm. It must have been July – perhaps August. The wild strawberries come in a bit later that far north. They also come in later as one heads to higher elevations, like in the Rockies. I must have been eight or ten years old and on summer holidays. For whatever reason, it was a good year for wild strawberries. Granny and I set out with pails, the old gallon-sized buckets in which ice cream was sold. The strawberry patch was on a gentle, northwest slope in a pasture grazed by the cows, not far from a fence that divided the cleared land from the trembling aspen and birch woods. The air smelled of strawberries. The air rustled the trees. Cows lowed every now and again. It was quiet. My memory is simply of quiet, of sitting amidst the strawberries, picking them one by one, each berry smaller than my pinky fingernail. Bit by bit, they filled the bucket. At one point a cow came over to check on us and gave me a gentle nudge. Granny was nearby. I don't remember any of what we said, or if we said anything at all. I remember the sound of berries in the pail, set against the quiet of a warm afternoon. The pleasure of finding a plump, ripe berry hiding under a leaf stands in for the plenitude of childhood. Perhaps Granny made a strawberry-rhubarb pie. Perhaps she made jam. I don't remember. Instead, I remember a simple, still day. It was a day made remarkable only by the passage of time and the progression, through the days of warmth, from shoot to plant to berry to tongue. The memory is a way out from the concrete of the everyday. It points toward a possible tomorrow, too, one of warmth and soil.

❧

When my eldest child was very young, we took her to visit the family doctor whose attention we had managed to secure. She was then new and pink, tiny fingers not yet clasping. I was worried that any move might harm her small, delicate digits and downy-soft fontanelle. Telling the doctor about our family's medical history, I mentioned that two of my grandparents – one on either side, Granny and my maternal grandfather – had died of brain tumours. In both cases, they died at relatively young ages. The doctor asked me where and how they had lived. I told her that they had lived on farms in northern Alberta. Pesticides, herbicides, chemicals, the doctor suggested. I didn't – and don't – know better than she did. We could argue the science of it, as people do. Yet the idea was a new one to me. It was a fresh way to look at a long-examined problem. It helped me to start to put to rest my own anxiety about inheriting brain cancer, though of course that fear lingers.

ꙮ

I love the farms and fields of northern Alberta, set amidst the forests. Yet what toxins are out there, lurking in the pastures and croplands, the environments that I associate with pastoral imagery? These are the calmest, most serene and seemingly purest landscapes. In many cases, however, they are also highly polluted, awash with chemicals. While the mix of chemicals has changed over the years since Rachel Carson wrote *Silent Spring* and brought forth a public awareness of the impacts of DDT, the fields are far from unsullied.

ꙮ

Years later, we managed to take a family trip to Athabasca. It was the first for my two young children. We drove up north of the river, past the site of the Big Coulee country store that I remember my great-grandmother still running when I was young and then past the old farm. Driving on a back road near that farm, my mother asked me to stop the car so that she could take pictures of the boarded up Ukrainian Orthodox church. It was derelict, its modest countryside onion domes a surprise only for those who don't know the settlement patterns of this place. The small church on the side of the road, next to a field and a stand of trees, was now beginning its own slow collapse. We unloaded from the car, my eldest setting down her book and following her grandmother. My younger child, ever mischevious, bolted instead through the unfenced field, barley stalks turning golden in the sun. My mother turned her camera toward the field and running child. I brought my children to the edge of the field, endeavouring to show them what barley was; how you can identify its soft, grainy heads; how the seeds crack sweetly in one's teeth.

ʒ

Only thereafter, as we headed back to the car, did I have a realization: the field was void of any other growth but that of perfect, beautiful, knee-high barley stalks. They grew in their upright rows and stretched out against the sun. There is only one way to achieve such consistent beauty: chemical application. A course of herbicides and pesticides. The uniformity of the growth and the sheer weedlessness were both signs of a crop that was genetically modified to withstand a defoliant that kept every other plant from so much as sprouting, as well as of the application of a defoliant such as glyphosate.

ʒ

Such fields are doubtless wonderful to look at. Have you ever stood in one? I suggest that you do so sometime. At first look – from the window of a car, for instance – the fields are glorious. Barley, wheat, canola, flax wave from the side of the road. Waves of wind wash over the shores of the grasses. If you stop the car, you can hear the gentle sound of the plants' stirring. Listen and you can hear the rustle of grasses rubbing against one another. But go closer. The plants are so uniform, so perfect. There's the rub. Stand in the field. All of a sudden your boots are getting dirty. In the fields of my own childhood, sure, there was dirt and mud, but there was also ground cover. There was chickweed, say, or alfalfa sneaking in below. Maybe foxtail, clover, vetch, fescue. Forbs. I think of the strawberry field, coming back time and again, a low network of leaves and runners, flowers and berries. Yet there is no ground cover in this field now. Nor in many of the fields in which you might stop. The seeds that are grown are modified. They are designed to withstand special chemicals that wipe out everything else. Yields are maximized, nature is minimized. At ground level, there is nothing, just weakening soil. It is a soil that is leaching its nutrients into the air and into the water table, along with the chemicals that it bears. To the farmer, the purity and quality of the crop might mean profit in a tight market that is getting tighter by the minute. Fewer contaminating plants and better grain means more money in the bank. It might mean no foreclosure this year. Yet it might also mean worsening soil, the need for more chemical fertilizers next year and a new loan to get the fields growing again. The beautiful fields, you soon realize, are not in a good way. They are suffering, even if it is a splendid suffering, as the breeze greets you with the sound of a quiet late summer's content.

⟨

We headed back to the car. I vowed to wash my children that evening. I said nothing then, but we discussed it later, over the dinner table. We concluded that it couldn't have been much to fuss over. We don't live on that land or work those fields. But others do, human and more-than-human neighbours all linked together.

⟨

Driving back to town, we crossed the river. The river defines the town – or at least my relationship to it. I try to be attuned to the moods of the seasons and of the times. The river and how it shapes the town, as well as my thinking of it, sticks in my mind. When my parents were born, this bridge had just been built. It was shiny with possibilities. The ferry and cable car had all become obsolete. The bridge, the local newspapers claimed, would open the road to the north and to the future. There was a parade and a festival. It's not unreasonable to think that my parents might never have met had the bridge not been built. Infrastructure and daily lives and the trees all around, impacted by concrete and steel.

ʒ

I often walked along the river with Grandma June when I visited town. She has been a widow and a pensioner for the duration of my life, that is, after her husband died and she sold the farm on the north side of the bridge. We would walk down to the river, perhaps along it, toward the aspens, if the mosquitoes weren't bad. Then up past the post office on the way back home. I would struggle to understand what the bridge must have meant, looking at it from the riverfront. The forests on the north side of the river were thick. It can still feel desolate to me, far away from town yet very close. My grandfather used to drive the school bus that took the kids to the small rural school. He also operated the tiny rural postal outlet where letters would come from the old countries – Poland, the USSR, France, the UK, Ireland, Czechoslovakia, East and West Germany and more. I have an old stamp collection gathered from those letters around here somewhere. The community was hewn from the land and the cold and from hanging on, hanging on together, until the next harvest, until it was time to cart the crops across the ferry – and later the bridge – to the old grain elevator.

ʒ

I think of dogs and coyotes baying back and forth in the farm's night air. Or else I think of the different sounds of lowing that cows make in different seasons. I think of aspen leaves – birch, alder and willow too – rustling in the wind. Machinery in the fields, the *pip-pip* of gophers, the screams of hawks on the wind. The calm voices of grown-ups around me, laughter, conversation, coffee and cups. The sighing and groaning of the trunks of spruces and aspens in the forest. These are all sounds that come to me in the evenings as I nod off to sleep, even still.

≀

Most of all, the sound of a winter's night. Many people have described the sounds of the universe. Dante, exiled from his fourteenth-century Florence, described the celestial music of the Godhead in part three of his *Divine Comedy*. In this book, the pilgrim Dante takes leave of his guide Virgil at the top of Mount Purgatory. He then proceeds on a guided tour through the Empyrean, imagined as the vast celestial orbits beyond the earth. Book three – *Paradise* – is considerably duller than books one and two – *Inferno* and *Purgatory* – because depicting the suffering of sinners has much greater narrative pull than a very long description of everything being perfect in Heaven. Yet the celestial music of the heavens that Dante describes stuck with me. Leonard Cohen, in his novel *Beautiful Losers*, has Catherine Tekakwitha describe her priest's voice as "ordinary eternal machinery like the grinding of the stars," a line that has stuck with me also. I remember transcribing from both books into a notebook that I kept as a moody teenager, seeking words that would comfort and console me. *The Divine Comedy* and *Beautiful Losers* remain books that I have continued to visit. To me, the night air was not quite the celestial music that Dante celebrated, nor was it ordinary eternal machinery, grinding away up there. But both descriptions captured something. The night air in mid-winter crackles with the sounds of a wide, vibrant universe. In the cold, the air ripples with the sounds of static electricity – my sister and I, as besocked children, dragging our feet across the carpets in Grandma's living room in order to shock each other, the blue light jumping from our fingertips. But the night skies stretched far beyond that. Outside, the howl of the wind and the yawning gulp of the night air, the expanse of it rushing down the land on which Granny and Grandpa's farmhouse stood. The noise of vistas, the million stars of a dark, clear night, far from any source of light (though one light was kept on in the farmyard). Darkened silhouettes of the forests, outlines pointing their way toward the stars. The stars waver, and we can imagine their sound only at a remove, a slow dispersal of sound waves disappearing across the universe and the impossible vacuum of space. Or the aurora. The inversion of gases over the pole tumbling, falling in greens through the night sky, white-purpling at the edges. It sounds, in my mind, like a shimmering tear rent in the fabric of the night. A slow descending scale of icy tinkling, sotto voce, pianissimo; the heavens tuned to a register just beyond my hearing.

{

What happens when we think of the sky as having sound rather than colour? In itself it has neither – or perhaps both. When I take listening as seriously as I take sight, things shift. For me, it takes the rush of a cold winter's night – the darkness after the moon sets, before the sun rises – in order to restore hearing, in order to place listening at the centre of my attention. Listening takes time. It is slower to process, and is therefore a challenge to the world of speed. Listening to the night sky in the northern half of Alberta, in other words, is an act of deliberate slowness. It is a gift that I have been granted by the place.

{

It is warm today, unseasonably so. The radio announcers on the CBC are irritating me again by describing the weather as "great" and "wonderful." It is winter. The aspens outside shiver into themselves, while the spruces and pines hunch their shoulders into their parkas of green needles in anticipation of snow. It should be cold. Beautiful weather means minus ten to minus twenty temperatures and a fresh layer of snow at this time of year.

ξ

My expectations for the weather were built from my childhood experiences. As winter carries on, I think of Boxing Day on the farm. Each year, it brought together my surviving grandparents on both sides of the family; my immediate family; as many of my father's four brothers as were able to be home for the season, along with their families; and some of the neighbours. Having spent Christmas in their own homes, the families would gather for a shared celebration. The day was Granny's continuation of an older tradition, when we used to visit her mother's home, a rambling old bungalow in Edmonton that was surrounded by caragana, on Boxing Day. That tradition passed with my great-grandmother. At the farm, there was food aplenty: turkey, ham and pies. Adults floated about upstairs, helping in the kitchen. The upstairs living room was the space for the adults. It was sparsely decorated with minimal leather couches, an easy chair and the stereo. The stereo, in my memory at least, played Christmas music from the turntable or else was off. What art there was consisted of Indigenous carvings and prints from up north. My aunts and uncles, my grandparents and the neighbours spread out across the kitchen, dining table and living room. Coffee mugs were perpetually refilled. Low winter light filled the space as the sun rose and dipped along the horizon. The basement was the space for the children. It was darker down there. The door banged every now and again when another person came in or went out. There was a growing pile of snowy boots and heavy coats. Cold air poured in when the door opened. My cousins and my sister and I rifled through my grandparents' bookcases and pulled games out of the basement storage – the shelves on which the old bleached skulls and bones were also kept. We would step into the cold room and pull out bottles of pop – Tahiti Treat, Canada Dry. We played with the old plastic figurines and the few toy cars. The basement could only contain us for so long. The trees were calling. Sooner or later, we would put on our snow pants, boots, coats, mittens and toques. We'd head outside. The dogs followed us around. We would scamper around the woodpiles, through the hay bales, past the falling down barn and out to the paddock with the soft-lowing cattle. At some point, the adults would come outside too. We would all go tobogganing, heading to the old cut-road that ran down a hill a couple of farms over. The sled track was long, straight and lined with aspens and birches. It descended into the Tawatinaw Valley. The most epic slides were those of my father and his brothers. They careened down the hill together on the largest sled. As five full-grown farm boys, their momentum was considerable. Although this part of the tradition lasted only a few years and was curtailed by some bone-breaking injuries, it was a vibrant way to expend an afternoon's energies. The sun stretched out in its low winter angle, casting long shadows.

⁂

I recall the sound of walking back to the farm, a dog clipping at my heels. It was an attentive quiet that contrasted with my family's reverie. The cold, crisp snows muffled the sounds beyond our own, just as the sun reflected off the white layer on the ground. The trees provided some small echoes, our sounds bouncing from the trunks and bare branches. There were a few birds, but not many at this time of year. The sun set very early – around four o'clock at the winter solstice. Back at the farmhouse, the adults brought the food to the table for everyone to serve themselves, buffet style. The adults held their plates on their knees upstairs. We children ate our turkey, potatoes and gravy around the low coffee table in the basement. People lingered and visited. As the evening began to wear on, we piled into our car and drove back to town, to Grandma's house for the night. The wonderful weather, the beauty of a winter's day, followed up by the celestial motions of the cold night. Those moments of chill, of quiet, of glasses steaming up upon re-entering the house, the screen door clattering shut behind me. Great weather – cold, bright and boisterous.

{

Being isolated in a small, rural community may lead one to feel vulnerable to the whims and moods of the environment. In my reading, I regularly encounter stories from elsewhere in Canada, the popular narratives that occur in southern media or the understandings of the land that have emanated from writers based in Toronto (a place that I love, but that is not here). Seldom do these narratives much resemble the land as I have experienced it. I just can't quite grant Margaret Atwood's view, for instance, of northern land as a malevolent force, where the best we can hope for is mere survival. There is a great deal of interconnection between those who live on the land, both with other people and with the non-humans who dwell in those spaces. Both of my parents – as well as my grandparents, uncles, aunts, cousins and more – have or had endless tales about life and its ties to the land. The tales displayed a land that was at times harsh, at time humorous and always one that you couldn't just oppose or defy. You had to work with it, as best you could.

{

My mother's family farm, which tumbled down to the banks of the Athabasca River, was one time subject to a forest fire. The fire was at first on the south side of the river. It raged for some time. The family watched it from across the water until it jumped the river and burned out a patch of woods near the water's edge. Fire was in this moment animate, live, jumping as a leggy toddler might across a rivulet. It was far from a contained and knowable thing that humans might control. Another time, a tornado – rare but not unheard of in that region – rushed through. As it approached, my great-grandmother – the one who ran the Big Coulee country store next to the old Anglican church on a small dirt road – fell to the floor, hoping for shelter from the twister. It landed right next to the house. It picked up a building across the way, which was never seen again, but it spared her. And then, as tornadoes do, it skipped off into the air. About forty kilometres to the south, about fifty metres from where my father's parents would later build their new farmhouse, a patch of trees had been similarly plucked from their tops down by a tornado. I always liked to imagine that it was that same rare weather event, taking up the garage to the north and then skirting town, touching down again to the south. A strange weather phenomenon to link the two families. I visited the bare patch often and marvelled at the forces that could dismantle the forest from the treetops down.

⁊

And then there was the beaver that bit one of the cows on Mom's farm and wouldn't let go. Its teeth clamped onto the cow's face. John, the finger-lacking farmhand, killed the beaver with a shovel. When they contacted animal control so that the beaver – and by extension the cow – could be checked for rabies, they were asked to keep the beaver until someone could come for it. So they kept it in the freezer for some time, its beaver-ish form haunting the farm's icebox. (The beaver turned out not to be rabid.) The stories move, the relations shift – it is about land and its inhabitants, the people become only some among the many who dwell there.

⁊

Stories arrive when the time is right. An important one from my grandmother didn't arrive until the pandemic. It was then, I suppose, that I was ready to hear it. In the early 1950s northern Alberta was struck with an outbreak of polio. That much I knew before. Members of my family were affected by the illness. There is also the section of the graveyard that I mentioned earlier, the section where children are buried. Many of them died during that outbreak. The story that I hadn't heard came over the phone, during one of the phone calls with Grandma that we held with greater frequency during the lockdowns. She had become a mother during the outbreak. There weren't many ways of preventing the illness. So Grandma stayed home. It was sure an awful time, was what she said. That was about it. She stayed home on the farm for two years. She had little human company besides her husband. Between her words, I hear the voices of the aspens, their whistling leaves in the breeze. I hear the cattle in the fields. I hear the loneliness of a new mother in her twenties – and the fortitude of an enduring woman now in her mid-nineties, seventy-some years later, recalling the stillness with certainty. Perhaps thinking of the sky on a cool morning on the farm, fog rolling from the Athabasca River.

⸘

The farm north of the river was translated, after my grandfather's death, into my grandmother's small, stuccoed house in town. It was the house in which I spent many of my childhood Christmases. Boxing Days on my paternal grandparents' farm, Christmases with my maternal grandmother. Three days, more or less, of the biting cold, the voice of the winter wind and the static crackle – and then back to the city.

⸘

Grandma's house was a dark old house with corners that I left unexamined for fear of spiders. Under the stairs to the basement there was a patch of dirt floor, a door opening to paint cans and potatoes stored next to one another. That space smelled earthy. The kitchen held cupboards piled high with dishes. Tins of food stood in the cupboards, back in the era that predated expiry dates. Mom leaned into the sink and did the dishes, cooked. Dad helped to repair things. Grandma saved up some chores that I could help with: fence posts in need of repainting, burned-out light bulbs, loose screws, things in the garage. Depending on the season, I would be asked to mow the lawn or shovel the snow. For me and my sister, it was a somewhat foreboding yet warm home. The bunks in the basement, separated, held us in our sleep. The walls were cold and wood panelled. I peeled the shellac off the wall next to the bed in order to forestall the inevitability of rising from the old mattress's cool embrace. I had to climb back out of the bed in the morning, my warm feet hitting the chilly linoleum.

≀

The house was never far from the land, and never far from giving evidence of my grandfather's and my aunt's passing. Their ghosts were everywhere, even though they had lived out their time on the farm. Grandma kept their things, including their clothes. A room in the basement was devoted to disused things saved for future needs. Many of these things had been theirs. My aunt, who died at the age of sixteen, seemed ever-present. Her death haunted – haunts – my family. My grandmother's life was irrevocably impacted by this death, close in time to her husband's. My experience of it was ghostly. My aunt's clothing in the basement. Her picture on the mantle. Her plaques from the town piano competitions on the wall. When I visited alone, I sometimes stayed in the office-slash-guest-room on the main floor of the bungalow. This room held an overfull desk as well as a bed piled high with blankets. The closet contained I knew not what. The room felt perpetually twilit, even when the sunlight struck the sheers that covered the narrow window. To me the menace, the terrifying menace, was my aunt's stuffed Tasmanian Devil from the *Looney Tunes* cartoons. It scared me for reasons that I could neither place nor articulate. It was a feature of my nightmares, a malevolent reminder that the cheerful life of a child can quickly become a pall of loss.

⸖

Yet I loved the house and its environs. Across the street from Grandma's, aspen woods climbed the hillside. The flatlands immediately opposite had been cleared and were a mix of flowers and grasses. Behind these was the hill, with its pathway straight up that doubled as a toboggan run in winter. All else was forest. The trees, never silent, but quiet, watched over me. At the end of the block on which the house stood one could cross the street in any direction and be amidst the forests, pathways through the trees well-established but not quite frequented.

⸖

The trees have taught me many things. I gravitate toward them, heading out from the edge of town or the beginning of a trailhead. In a recent early summer, we were hiking in the backwoods near Jasper. This adventure was one of our family attempts to find the stars. It was the second day of our hike and we were at least ten kilometres from any roads. We hadn't seen any other people in the early summer drizzle, though we had seen plenty of mosquitoes. The trees reached skyward. Our toes dampened in the soft earth of the trail. Some time near lunchtime, we heard a rustling. Then came a series of *peep! peep!* sounds from birds nearby. All of a sudden, the ground seemed to be moving. The dog's ears went back and I paused. We soon realized what it was. About two metres off the path, a mother grouse stood in the low willow and alder scrub. Her sharp eyes glared at us. The brush seemed to be moving because of her brood of young. All six or seven of them were exploring the forest floor. They made delicate, uncertain sounds as they went. I guessed that they had never encountered people before – not the chicks, at any rate, which could only have been a few days old. While they seemed uncertain, they didn't seem to be afraid, either. The mother bird watched us all. We stopped and watched them, too. A chick stepped out of the thicket and onto the overgrown path. It was heading toward its mother, presumably in search of protection, comfort. It was very small and would have fit easily, cupped, into the palm of my hand, I thought for a moment. If you have ever seen such birdlings, you will know. This young bird's feathers were downy and its call was soft too. It looked back at the mother bird. I recalled another mountain adventure when I was about sixteen. That time, two friends and I were attacked by a similar bird that was defending its trailside nest. That was on another mountain, surrounded by different trees, near Moraine Lake. We fled in a hurry that time. There is no telling what an angry grouse may do. I looked down and saw, in the moment that it takes to blink, the dog lean down, sniff a birdling and pop it into his mouth. Our dog was then a puppy, though already a good size. He was brought home to us from a nearby humane society. Of undetermined breed, he grew into a very large, black and furry hound with a white patch on his chest. He yowled like a wolf when young, has always appeared to be at least part retriever and has held onto the herding instincts of a border collie. And, at this moment, he had a baby bird in his mouth. He looked up at me, his eyes seeming to say, "Now what do I do?" In his mouth, the grouse's peeps started to sound very alarmed. Without thinking about it, I reached down, took the dog by his muzzle with one hand and opened his mouth with the other. The delicate chick fell out and into my hand. I deposited it on the other side of the trail. Seemingly unhurt, it scampered off through some dogwood – or bunchberry – flowers and into the brush, toward its mother. The dog looked at me again. This time his look was sheepish or perhaps embarrassed. Just like our exchanges with the planet, I thought for a moment. We hold nature in our clutches, in our maw, not knowing how to hold it tenderly, how to care for it. How like children or puppies we can be, looking around for guidance, for someone to tell us that it's okay – all the while knowing that perhaps this time it will not be. As she moved off into the forest, the mother grouse kept her eye on us. She looked sharply at me. The message that I took was that, this time, she would let us pass. But she kept watch. I nodded in recognition. We continued, the dog hanging his head as we went.

{

My time on the land extends as I write the field notes that become this project. One day, I took a break from my table in order to sit in the brilliant, warm sun. It was one of those late-season days of warmth that we get in Calgary. I had spent too long editing, sitting at my screen, straining both my eyes and my concentration. The sun lighted the land and cast wild shadows across the Weaselhead Flats. I sat there and wrote. I have been coming to this place for thirty-some years now. I have watched the land change across the seasons and across the decades. My parents first took me here, but I have been exploring on my own for a long time now. In the last decade, I have brought my own children here in turn. How to approach this land well? I think of an offering from the poet a.rawlings, whose interactions with different landscapes inspire me. In her instructional poetic piece "How to Have a Conversation with a Place" rawlings writes:

1. Learn about the landscape before you enter into it.
2. Begin by introducing yourself.
3. Be aware of your inner monologue.
4. Listen.
5. Be genuinely interested.
6. Give the landscape time to think and respond.
7. Synchronize.
8. Maintain the equilibrium.
9. Know when the conversation is over.
10. Practice having conversations.

While I first learned about this land in a more haphazard, youthful way than she advocates, Weaselhead is nonetheless a place that I have come to admire and respect across our many conversations. On this particular day, the land was quiet. Dried leaves rustled on the poplars, or else they scraped against each other on the ground. Chickadees called and chattered, while the swallows that nest on the underside of the new bridge had moved on for the winter. The bridge crosses the Elbow River just above where it enters the Glenmore Reservoir, one of the city's main water sources. I startled a juvenile red squirrel with my movements. It skittered off into the understorey. The day remained calm and serene. Blue skies lay above the spruces in front of me. The forest smelled of decaying leaves and humus while the river, at a low ebb, moved on.

≀

Yet the Weaselhead is a land disrupted. Someone hammered away, perhaps as far as the neighbourhood of Lakeview. I remembered Al Purdy's poem about someone hammering away across Roblin Lake. Then I also heard a leaf blower. Most of all, I heard the sounds of construction – the building of the new southwest extension of Calgary's ring road. As if the land didn't already have enough to worry about. On my way here were familiar warnings about unexploded ordnance, from when this place was on the edge of a military firing range that was on the edge of the Tsuut'ina Nation's reserve. I saw a couple of cautions about underground gas pipelines as well as one about whirling disease in the fish. There are also invasive plant species – buckthorn, Siberian pea, honeysuckle, knapweed – that are choking the willows and aspens. Now, the construction on the ring road has – even if only temporarily – cut off wildlife access to the Tsuut'ina reserve to the west. Bears, deer, coyotes, beavers, muskrats and many smaller species are all affected. According to city officials and planners, the ring road construction will not permanently damage the Weaselhead. I wish I could believe that. The politics of the ring road have been complicated enough just for the humans to endeavour to sort out. The frogs and diving beetles and harvestmen are all without voice as humans usually understand it, so their pleas go unanswered. It's been a many-year-long negotiation between the City of Calgary, the Province of Alberta and the Tsuut'ina Nation. The eventual agreement has seen a package of funding and new lands transferred to the nation. These are the complex nation-to-nation negotiations in what many currently call Canada. The interhuman challenges are far from sorted out, but they are, by the time of my listening, literally in the process of being paved over in the name of progress. My own inkling is that more roads simply lead to more traffic – which leads to more roads. The infrastructure is unsustainable in the long run, but that has too seldom stopped humans from doing things. Local advocates for the Weaselhead may sigh and shake their heads.

⁊

How should we interact with the land? I think of Robin Wall Kimmerer and her articulation of the "Honorable Harvest." Kimmerer doesn't oppose sharing the land with our fellow species. Instead, she provides a way that we might think about how to share – how to harvest – in a way that returns to the land what is taken. Here is how Kimmerer puts it:

> Know the ways of the ones who take care of you, so that you may take care of them.
> Introduce yourself. Be accountable as the one who comes asking for life.
> Ask permission before taking. Abide by the answer.
> Never take the first. Never take the last.
> Take only what you need.
> Take only that which is given.
> Never take more than half. Leave some for others.
> Harvest in a way that minimizes harm.
> Use it respectfully. Never waste what you have taken.
> Share.
> Give thanks for what you have been given.
> Give a gift, in reciprocity for what you have taken.
> Sustain the ones who sustain you and the earth will last forever.

The parallels with a.rawlings's instructions are striking to me, even though settler conservation and Indigenous harvest are two distinct things. Can we develop a way of caring for and returning to the land? For Kimmerer, writing is one way of respecting the gifts that she has received from the land. Kimmerer writes: "For me, writing is an act of reciprocity with the world; it is what I can give back in return for everything that has been given to me." Returning the gifts of the land, however, is a lengthy, slow process. When I was young, I learned to bike in the Weaselhead. Biking off the pavement has been prohibited here for the past twenty-odd years, but it was allowed back then. I have strong memories of biking under the trees, over the roots and through the mudholes. I recall riding into what looked like a small puddle only to find myself pitched headfirst into waist-deep mud. My father took the garden hose to me when I got home.

I remember, too, fording the river when the old bridge had washed out. I held my bike above my head, chest-deep water chilling me as the rocks underfoot slipped in the springtime current. I wobbled, stayed on my feet and made it across. I learned to respect the water. I remember the trails in all seasons. I think of the times I brought my children here to explore the trees and birds and swamp water. I think of the field trip with my elder child where we found a spider as big as my hand. Warblers, cedar waxwings, red-winged blackbirds.

⁊

I came to the Weaselhead one time with a fellow writer who was visiting the city. She was writing about urban forests. We started at the parking lot on the north side of the reservoir and then descended into the trees. As we walked, we sought out the fungi in the woods, so we headed toward the south side of the flats. On that side of the woods, the hillside provides more ground cover and there is a thicker understorey. We found mushrooms in some abundance, strolled, spoke about how to write well and with respect of such places. We paused and listened. What was most remarkable to me was seeing the Weaselhead from another perspective, one that sought parallel features of the forest, all under the canopy of learning to think environmentally.

⁊

The Weaselhead was likely named for a Tsuut'ina chief, as the City of Calgary acknowledges and as local writer Jesse Salus has explored in some depth. The details of the history are complicated, as is the place itself. The area exists as a well-used nature reserve now, but the seeming historical gaps may parallel the land's future destruction at the hands of urban development. What could our listening to the land do to protect it, hold it against a future of becoming another paved paradise? On my walk with my fellow writer, we spotted a stand of poplars next to a pond. The trees were wrapped in wire cages. The cages were designed to dissuade beavers. What might dissuade the people?

⁊

Maybe you, like me, are tired of the noise. (If you accept that old distinction between noise and sound, which many academics don't.) Maybe you are tired of the disquiet. Or of the lack of opportunity to be well and truly with yourself. To be honest, I listen well to the world only in fits and starts, in the moments between things when I can witness spaces of quiet and when I can hear the land. I work at it – and it is work. It comes from spending a long time listening to difficult stories and then learning to cease expecting there to be simple, straightforward answers. I work to hear the sounds of the forest and then to provide language that would translate those things into something meaningful here on the page with the idea that knowing, recording and witnessing these things might make them somehow valuable, something to hold onto.

⁊

In the end, the land on which I stand, as well as the land to the north, the land around Athabasca, has taught – and continues to teach – me many things. I learned these things slowly, to whatever extent I have indeed learned anything at all. Listening to the wind, the water and the leaves, as well as those who have loved me enough to guide me along, from my family and friends to the dogs and the cows, has taught me. Listening is bounded by time. Rather than an image or a word that can be glimpsed at speed, listening proceeds as the moments unfold. Perhaps that is why it makes a solid metaphor for thinking and learning. Without the time to reflect, we will not be able to find ways to change. The future is temporal: what we do with it will be up to us. I'll be listening. I'll be stepping off the sidewalks at the end of Grandma's street and heading into the trees, finding the paths and discovering what there is to hear.

≀

A final story from the land. Before I ever read or heard a coyote story, and well before names like Thomas King were on my literary radar, I grew up knowing coyotes as part of life. They were a constant presence on the land. They gave nightly performances from the trees behind the farmhouse, out past the garden and over the wire fence. They impressed themselves on me. They came out of the woods, just to their very edge, and began singing in an effort, it seemed, to drive the dogs to distraction. The dogs always responded. Their loud barks were a warning to the coyotes to back off and leave the chickens and the sheep alone. There was a territorial, geographical posturing to it. The coyotes began in the trees – one could look out and see their gleaming eyes – while the dogs ran around on the deck. As the howling and the barking escalated, the coyotes might venture up to the fence. The dogs would go to the edge of the garden. The garden served as a seeming demilitarized zone between the factions. If there were incursions, the howls, yips and barks escalated. My grandfather might at this point get a gun and fire a blank into the night to disperse the coyotes. Then a ceasefire on all sides would ensue. From the basement room in which I slept when I stayed on the farm, I would listen, enraptured, at length falling asleep.

≀

By daylight, however, it was a different situation. One summer when I must have been twelve or so, I took my favourite dog, a vivacious border collie, for a mid-afternoon walk out to the back quarter section by myself. To get there, one left the farmhouse, crossed the garden – stepping on the flagstones so as not to sink into the loose, airy loam – and then passed through the stile in the fence. On the other side of the barbed wire, the cattle grazed through the aspen forest. Wavering paths forged by their hooves crossed the glade and wound around the trees. A wider path – a dirt road for the tractor – bisected the trees. This path was the one that I followed, listening for the dog, who ran off into the undergrowth. She came back at intervals to check on me, then sped off again. On some walks she might find a good stick, or an old bone, or perhaps a dead bird. Burrs, seeds and twigs caught in her black-and-white fur. Down the path, pasture land opened onto a hillside, backstopped by the animal graveyard and the boreal forest beyond. The pasture sloped away from me, turning from green to gold in the ripening summer. Shadows were beginning to lengthen. Across the field, a clutch of coyotes stood at the edge of the forest in the daylight. They watched our progress, mine and the dog's. They didn't move from their spots, perhaps a hundred metres distant. They must have been downwind at first because the dog didn't notice them. Then she did. At first, her ears went back. She snarled. She barked. But the coyotes only offered playful yips in response. They came closer, bounding along in the field. They started a game of chase with one another. The dog's ears relaxed. I trusted her without reservation. To my surprise, she joined the coyotes. They added her to their game. They ran close, close enough that I might have touched each of the handful of coyotes gambolling with the dog on that warm hillside in the afternoon. A temporary truce, a suspension of hostilities. By night the howling and barking would resume, but, for the moment, a brief span of peace. The fields sounded different.

❧

The sounds of the north: What does the raw information of a seismic blast resemble? Is there a bird in this Rorschach? Perhaps it is a trumpeter swan or a whooping crane. Egrets, snowy owls, the birds that nest along the forests and the snowy tundra when these lands hit their highest temperatures in August, September, before the snows return. Or else we hear the vibrations of oil, gas, shale, rock. In a trailer set out on the land, somewhere north in my mind, my grandfather still sits, smoking, a round of cribbage, a cold night. Days spent setting charges – set the line, detonate, record, repeat. The blast reverberating, generating the data of seismic refraction. Were these the source of his failing hearing? Or was it the interminable rattle of the tractor's throttle and clutch? If we work the land too hard, do we lose our ability to listen, both literally and metaphorically? The snowcat moves across the ice road, a new day's destination. The crew – the dynamiters, seismographers, line runners and more – crash into sleep. A new reading, a subterranean vibration coming back with each blast. Each blast allows for a new mapping, the underground perceived – heard – and transmitted back to the surface. The goal was what it always seemed to be: oil. The ground's deposits register in lines, wisps, the ripples refracting back off of each element with its own particular signature. Careful listening allows one to see farther than vision ever might. And yet, late in her book *The Mushroom at the End of the World*, Anna Lowenhaupt Tsing writes: "How . . . shall we make common cause with other living beings? Listening is no longer enough; other forms of awareness will have to kick in. And what great differences yawn!" We will need to find ways to bring the possibility of that tricky verb, *listen*, together with other perceptions and verbs: *see, taste, smell – feel*.

❧

The third and most recent date on the bottom of our dining-room table is 2019, when one of our dearest and most brilliant friends – a carpenter and musician – disassembled and rebuilt the table once more. He removed some of the metal that held the old, evermore creaky table together and replaced it with wooden fittings. He also built a third leaf to match the other two, again for our expanding household and our pre-pandemic habits of hospitality. He finished the wood, also, to a waxy, lustrous shine. No more oiling needed, just very occasional waxing. The new leaf fits, yet it has the awkward distinction of being better-made than the rest of the works: its tight lamination, precise bevelling and sharp corners put the sighing, worn edges of the rest of the table into relief. I think of Roger Deakin's book *Wildwood*, in which he notes that contemporary carpenters expect squared precision in their work, whereas the Elizabethans who first built his home in the English countryside worked with the twists and yaws of the beams at hand. I find myself thinking that both approaches are probably correct in their own ways. I also anticipate how, after another hundred years of listening, the sag and give of the new leaf will line up beautifully with the rest of the table in worn-out splendour. I imagine future humans gathering around it to speak and to learn to listen to one another, telling tales of this time of the pandemic and how we endured. I lay my ear to the table, listening to the silence of the wood grain, a silence that is anything but quiet.

CODA

The sound of birds, not traffic, from the balcony.
The sound of physical distancing.
The sound of stimulus packages and bailouts.
The sound of ventilator shortages.
The sound of self-isolation.
The sound of spring.
The sound of my slow, steady pulse.
The sound of online video conferencing.
The sound of dance parties in the kitchen.
The sound of daily updates from the prime minister.
The sound of the news.
The sound of the children home from school.
The sound of walking the dog.
The sound of hand sanitizer.
The sound of everything being cancelled.
The sound of K-pop.
The sound of school from home.
The sound of keys jangling.
The sound of the first robins of spring.
The sound of the laundry machine, walking across the floor during
   the spin cycle.

The endless, endless sound of Donald Trump.

The sound of songbirds.

The sound of the dog asking to be taken out for another walk.

The sound of onions and garlic sautéing in the pan.

The sound of spring rains.

The sound of memes.

The sound of the same day stuck on repeat.

The sound of trees in bloom.

The sound of snow piles melting and riveting toward the storm drains.

The sound of medical professionals conducting press conferences.

The sound of the fiftieth anniversary of Earth Day.

The sound of springtime thunderstorms.

The sound of the United States' unravelling.

The sound of Black Lives Matter.

The sound of tentative reopening.

The sound of sunshine.

The sound of gardens.

The sound of curfews.

The sound of protest, rage and hurt.

The sound of fish jumping in the evening light.

The sound of a grouse defending her nest.

The sound of fireweed shoots.

The sound of a black bear up ahead on the trail.

The sound of keys clacking on keyboards.

The sound of a dog and coyote call-and-answer on solstice.

The sound of all of the cats, pissed off because the humans are still home.

The sound of a caress, a sigh.

The sound of stockpiling.

The sound of spruces creaking.

The sound of bated breath.

BY WAY OF BIBLIOGRAPHY

It is usual to acknowledge one's readerly and personal debts in books of this nature, and there are many ways to do so. But over the years, I have become more and more aware that the conventional methods can push readers away from a book just at the moment when the writer is trying to invite readers to follow up with the works that inspired the text. I am far from the first to acknowledge that this can be troubling, nor am I the first to recognize that different projects call for different approaches.

In this spirit, then, of offering readers ways into the various materials that inform this work, I offer this section by way of bibliography. I am inspired to do so by some specific recent texts, including Nora Samaran's *Turn This World Inside Out: The Emergence of Nurturance Culture*, published by AK Press in 2019; Cherokee scholar Daniel Heath Justice's *Why Indigenous Literatures Matter*, published by Wilfrid Laurier University Press in 2018; Erin Wunker's *Notes from a Feminist Killjoy: Essays on Everyday Life*, published by Book*hug in 2016; and Maggie Nelson's *The Argonauts*, published by Graywolf Press in 2015. Each of these books thinks about texts, references and citations in different ways. None of these books are comparable to this one, nor do I intend to compare my works to theirs. Rather, I would like to acknowledge a debt to these books and their writers for offering alternative ways of thinking about bibliographies.

In what follows, I acknowledge the specific texts and debts that occur in each section of this book. There are quite a few, and I have endeavoured to include them as much as I am able, while giving readers a brief sense of why each reference pops up. After putting this book together for several years, tracking down these references entailed an enjoyable romp through my mental bookshelves as I endeavoured to recall where I had stored each of these titles – some upstairs, some downstairs, some lost, some in boxes. Three specific points of inspiration, though, precede my sharing the details below. This book takes important cues from Ariel Gordon's *Treed: Walking in Canada's Urban Forests*, Daniel Coleman's *Yardwork: A Biography of an Urban Place* and Jenna Butler's *A Profession of Hope: Farming on the Edge of the Grizzly Trail*. These books were published by Wolsak and Wynn, also the publisher of this present book, in the years 2019, 2017 and 2015 respectively. Wide-ranging reading and rereading of Sid Marty's works while I was editing the manuscript also proved to be inspiring. His book *Leaning on the Wind: Under the Spell of the Great Chinook*, published by HarperCollins in 1995, provides excellent insights into life in southern Alberta, and into the effects of chinook winds in particular. While I hope that it is evident, none of these writers, nor their texts, should be held responsible for any of my own work's shortcomings. These shortcomings are entirely my own.

A note on the epigraph to the book: Margaret Avison's poem "Butterfly Bones: Sonnet Against Sonnets" was originally published in 1960 and is reprinted in volume one of Avison's collected poems, *Always Now*, published by Porcupine's Quill in 2003. "Butterfly

Bones" uses the line "fierce listening," and that line inspired an important element of what I endeavour to do in this work.

PRELUDE

Only one specific text is referenced here: Virginia Woolf's novel *Jacob's Room*, published in 1922 by Hogarth. This section of the text (matched by the coda at the end of the book) consists of the specific sounds that I heard on a daily basis during the most intense period of writing this manuscript, between the beginning of January and the end of June 2020. This period of time coincided with the rise of the Covid-19 pandemic, though hardly by design. I read *Jacob's Room* for the first time during those months. Events mentioned in the prelude and coda that occurred within this window of time will be familiar to many.

I

The first epigraph is a quotation from Virginia Woolf and the second one is a line from an essay by John Cage. Woolf is a touchstone writer for me, and I return to her work often. This particular epigraph is a minor line from Woolf's gender- and genre-defying "biography" *Orlando*, a book whose final line comes to a rest on the date and hour of the book's publication in 1928 by Hogarth Press. John Cage's *Silence*, from which his line comes, is a book that will reappear in what follows. *Silence* was published in 1961 by Wesleyan University Press. Cage's stature as an experimental composer and performer is well-known; his enthusiasm for mycology perhaps less so. That he brings those things together in his work is something that I find delightful.

I open with brief references to the many dialogues attributed to the Greek philosopher Plato, who advanced a concept of ideal "forms" of things – like tables – that underlie the specific ones that we encounter in everyday life. I then mention Margaret Avison's "Butterfly Bones: Sonnet Against Sonnets," picking up on the book's epigraph. The section of text beginning with "When I was a younger version of me," and the two following sections were inspired by poet bpNichol's *Selected Organs: Parts of an Autobiography*, published by Black Moss Press in 1988. I published these sections, in a different form, in issue 1 of the *Belfield Literary Review*, and thank Gregory Betts and Lucy Collins for editing that work.

John Cage's *4'33"* is available in many performances online. My discussion comes from Cage's *Silence* as well as Kyle Gann's 2010 book *No Such Thing as Silence: John Cage's* 4'33", published by Yale University Press. While Cage's thinking and compositions are important to my thinking, so too is the complex and imperfect work of R. Murray Schafer. His book *The Tuning of the World*, published by McClelland & Stewart in 1977 contains, on page 99, the anecdote about correlations between electronic frequencies and meditative chanting. The critique of Schafer in xwélméxw scholar Dylan Robinson's *Hungry Listening: Resonant Theory for Indigenous Sound Studies*, published by University of Minnnesota Press in 2020, is something through which I am still thinking.

I move on to quote directly from Trevor Herriot's *Towards a Prairie Atonement*, published in 2016 by the University of Regina Press. The quotations come from pages 80 and 113. The second of these comes from Métis teacher Norman Fleury, who writes the book's afterword and accompanies Herriot on his travels. Kevin Van Tighem has written well and for a long time about Alberta and western Canada. I am thinking in particular of his most recent book, *Wild Roses Are Worth It: Reimagining the Alberta Advantage*, published by Rocky Mountain Books in 2021. Audre Lorde's line "your silence will not protect you" – often invoked as a rallying cry

– was delivered in a speech that became the essay "The Transformation of Silence into Speech and Action," and was then published in *The Cancer Journals* by Spinsters, Ink, in 1980.

St. Augustine's *Confessions* are often invoked in discussions of the history of reading. St. Augustine remains my favourite saint, and his life story, completed around the year 400, is among my touchstone texts. I've read, reread and thumbed through R.S. Pine-Coffin's 1961 translation in the Penguin Classics series often. Alberto Manguel's *A History of Reading*, published in 1998 by Vintage Canada, is one such book to invoke St. Augustine.

When I mention my birding book, the one to which I am referring is Chris Fisher and John Acorn's *Birds of Alberta*, published by Lone Pine in 1998. It is a very useful resource, though it was out of print for many years. I was glad to see a new edition published in 2020.

My copies of Granny's books by Danish philosopher Søren Kierkegaard – which remain on my shelves – are *Philosophical Fragments: Or a Fragment of Philosophy*, translated by David F. Swenson and published by Princeton University Press in 1936, and *Fear and Trembling* and *The Sickness Unto Death* bound as a single volume, both edited by Walter Lowrie, and also published by Princeton University Press, this time in 1941. Both books have price tags from the University of Alberta bookstore, where Granny most likely purchased them; the former cost $2.95, while the latter was $2.45. (The latter also bears Granny's signature on the flyleaf.)

Peter Wohlleben's *The Hidden Life of Trees*, translated by Jane Billinghurst, and published by Greystone Books in 2016, has been an international sensation, with numerous follow-up titles now in print. Rob Nixon's concept of "slow violence" has proven to be a tremendously versatile way of identifying environmental catastrophes – climate change and its many impacts – and comes from his book *Slow Violence and the Environmentalism of the Poor*, published by Harvard University Press in 2011.

My invocation of Adrienne Rich is linked to her speech – turned essay – called "Claiming an Education." I have taught it from her book *On Lies, Secrets, and Silence: Selected Prose, 1966–1978*, published by W.W. Norton in a revised edition in 1995.

The local history volume *Reflections from Across the River: A History of the Area North of Athabasca* was published in 1994 by the Northern Heights Historical Society, which was at that time a large group of folks. It clocks in at 915 folio pages and remains one of my best sources for local history.

When I mention the community of Amber Valley, I must note the limits to my ability to recount community stories, as Amber Valley has its own stories to tell. One book on the history of Black settlement in Alberta that I celebrate the publication of is *The Black Prairie Archives: An Anthology*, edited by Karina Vernon and published by Wilfrid Laurier University Press in 2020, which endeavours to make space for Black voices, historical and contemporary, from across the Prairies. I also recommend Bertrand Bickersteth's *The Response of Weeds: A Misplacement of Black Poetry on the Prairies*, published by NeWest Press in 2020.

Finally for this section, Pauline Oliveros's *Deep Listening: A Composer's Sound Practice*, was published in 2005 by iUniverse. I am most interested in her recordings, such as the 1989 album of the same title, created with Stuart Dempster and Panaiotis.

II

The first epigraph to this section comes from page 364 of Robert Macfarlane's 2019 book, *Underland: A Deep Time Journey* (I have the 2020 edition published by Penguin). The second, from Robert

Bringhurst and Jan Zwicky's *Learning to Die: Wisdom in the Age of Climate Crisis*, published by the University of Regina Press in 2018, is found on page 38 of that short, pithy book.

Chris Turner's book *The Patch: The People, Pipelines, and Politics of the Oil Sands*, published by Simon and Schuster in 2017, and Andrew Nikiforuk's *Tar Sands: Dirty Oil and the Future of a Continent*, published in a revised and updated edition by Greystone in 2010, can be read together for critical considerations of Alberta's oil industry.

Herbert Marcuse's *One-Dimensional Man* was published by Beacon Press in 1964; Paulo Freire's *Pedagogy of the Oppressed* was published in English, translated by Myra Bergman Ramos, in 1970 by Continuum; and Dr. Seymour Fisher's *Understanding the Female Orgasm* was published by Bantam in 1973. Granny's copy of Thomas King's *Green Grass, Running Water* was the 1994 Bantam Books paperback. George Ryga's *Ecstasy of Rita Joe* premiered in 1967 at the Vancouver Playhouse and was later published by Talonbooks in 1970. Ryga's biographer, James Hoffman, published *The Ecstasy of Resistance: A Biography of George Ryga* in 1995 with ECW Press; I take much of my guidance on Ryga from Hoffman's work. Michael Ondaatje's *In the Skin of a Lion*, published by McClelland & Stewart in 1987, has long been an important book to me.

Granny's master's thesis, "Learning from Each Other: The English Teacher on a Hutterite Colony," was defended at the University of Alberta in 1992.

George Bowering's "Never read my lines" comes from the poem "Summer Solstice" and has been reprinted in a few places, including *Changing on the Fly: The Best Lyric Poems of George Bowering*, published by Polestar / Raincoast in 2004. Thea Bowering responds in her book *Love at Last Sight*, published by NeWest Press in 2013. Warren Cariou's stunning essay "Going to Canada" was published as a foreword to the book *Across Cultures / Across Borders: Canadian Aboriginal and Native American Literatures*, a book co-edited by Paul DePasquale, Renate Eigenbrod and Emma LaRocque, published in 2009 by Broadview.

The English version of Jacques Derrida's long essay "The Animal That Therefore I Am (More to Follow)" was translated by David Wills and published in the journal *Critical Inquiry*, volume 28, number 2, in the winter of 2002. A book-length version followed in 2008 from Fordham University Press. I quote from pages 372 and 383 of the *Critical Inquiry* version. Nicole Shukin's book *Animal Capital: Rendering Life in Biopolitical Times* is among the books that address Derrida's essay. It was published in 2009 by the University of Minnesota Press. I lean also on Benoît Peeters's *Derrida: A Biography*, published by Polity in 2012, in this section of the text.

III

My first epigraph comes from Matthew Battles's thoughtful, compact book *Tree*, published by Bloomsbury in 2017. My second comes from Nan Shepherd's compelling book *The Living Mountain*, first published in 1977, which discusses her lifelong relationship with Scotland's Cairngorm Mountains. Robert Macfarlane praises Shepherd's book in his own writing and composed the introduction for the edition that I have, which was published by Canongate in 2014.

My discussion of Karl Marx's *Capital* specifically references volume one, pages 163 to 164 in my 1990 Penguin Classics edition, which was translated by Ben Fowkes and first published in 1976 – Marx's original was published in 1867.

Anthropologist Eduardo Kohn's *How Forests Think: Toward an Anthropology Beyond the Human*, published by the University of California Press in 2013, provides me with some important cues as I endeavour to think beyond anthropocentrism. When I mention caragana, I am thinking alongside literature scholar Sarah Krotz, who has thought deeply about this plant. I am also thinking through David Abram's book *Becoming Animal: An Earthly Cosmology*, published in 2010, though I have the 2011 Vintage edition; Robert Macfarlane's *Landmarks*, published by Hamish Hamilton in 2015, is equally key, particularly as I endeavour to return to the specificity of language that pertains to both trees and place. For the specific language of forests I am indebted to many, including Suzanne Simard's *Finding the Mother Tree: Discovering the Wisdom of the Forest*, published by Allen Lane in 2021. Henry David Thoreau's *Walden*, first published in 1854 – I have the Penguin Classics edition from 1983 – is a cornerstone of both American literature and environmental writing. I quote from page 7 of Charlotte Gill's *Eating Dirt: Deep Forests, Big Timber, and Life with the Tree-Planting Tribe*, published by Greystone in 2011.

Syilx Okanagan writer Jeannette Armstrong's 1998 essay "Land Speaking" was published in the book *Speaking for the Generations: Native Writers on Writing*, edited by Simon J. Ortiz and published by the University of Arizona Press. Dylan Robinson's book *Hungry Listening: Resonant Theory for Indigenous Sound Studies*, published by University of Minnesota Press in 2020, is a remarkable study. Robinson deliberately addresses settlers and Indigenous people as distinct audiences in the book, to the point of asking settler readers to not read certain portions of the text (a request by which I have abided).

Oji-Cree writer Joshua Whitehead has used the phrase "fierce listening" in a few places, including an interview with the Canadian Broadcasting Corporation in 2018, published online under the title "Joshua Whitehead explores Indigiqueer and two-spirit culture in his Canada Reads contending novel" on the CBC.ca website, as well as in the book *Making Love with the Land*, forthcoming with Knopf. My thanks to Joshua Whitehead for a consultation on his use of the term.

Translations of the Cree place names Meanook and Tawatinaw come from the document *Aboriginal Place Names*, a teaching resource published by the Government of Alberta. My citation of John Terpstra comes from page 7 of his book *Daylighting Chedoke: Exploring Hamilton's Hidden Creek*, published by Wolsak and Wynn in 2018. Robin Wall Kimmerer describes strawberries as a gift in her book *Braiding Sweetgrass: Indigenous Wisdom, Scientific Knowledge, and the Teachings of Plants*, published by Milkweed Editions in 2013. Kimmerer's book seems to be rapidly gaining the sort of classic status of Rachel Carson's *Silent Spring*, originally published in 1962 by Houghton Mifflin.

Dante Alighieri's three-part *Divine Comedy*, completed in the year 1320, is another of my touchstone texts, one that I leaf through often enough in its three volumes, and that I read first as a teenager, then again in university and then most recently when I arrived at the same age Dante was when he began his poetic journey, lost in the shaded forest. I rely on two editions: Dorothy L. Sayers's translation in the Penguin Classics series, published in 1949 (*Inferno*), 1955 (*Purgatory*) and 1962 (*Paradise*); and Allen Mandelbaum's parallel text edition with Bantam Classics, published in 1982, 1984 and 1986.

Leonard Cohen's 1966 novel, *Beautiful Losers*, was published by McClelland & Stewart in Canada and by Viking in the United States. Margaret Atwood advances views of the environment, to which I respond, in both *Survival: A Thematic Guide to Canadian Literature*, published by Anansi in 1972, and *Strange Things: The Malevolent North in Canadian Literature*, published by Oxford University Press in 1995.

a. rawlings's "How to Have a Conversation with a Place" appears as a short film on her website, arawlings.is. The film was created in 2016; previously the instructions appeared in print form on the same website. The Al Purdy poem to which I refer is titled "Wilderness Gothic," and it was originally published in the book *Wild*

Grape Wine, published in 1968 by McClelland & Stewart. It is often anthologized and I have taught it many times.

When I discuss the Weaselhead Flats and the southwest portion of Calgary's ring road construction, I would like to point readers to the documenting work of Jesse Salus on his website, calgaryringroad .com. The materials on which I rely are public news reports and my own experiences of the Weaselhead, but Salus's careful historical documentation deserves readers' further attention.

When I return to Robin Wall Kimmerer's *Braiding Sweetgrass*, I quote from pages 183 and 152 in my edition. Thomas King's particular characterization of coyote can be found in several places, but I think of his short story collection *One Good Story, That One*, published by HarperCollins in 1993, and the already-mentioned *Green Grass, Running Water*. Anna Lowenhaupt Tsing's *The Mushroom at the End of the World: On the Possibility of Life in Capitalist Ruins*, published by Princeton University Press in 2015, is a wonderful study of human-mushroom entanglements. I quote from page 254. Finally, Roger Deakin's wonderful, posthumously published book *Wildwood: A Journey Through Trees* was published by Hamish Hamilton in 2007; the anecdote to which I refer appears on pages 8 and 9 of my 2008 Penguin edition.

ACKNOWLEDGEMENTS

The acknowledgements in this book are difficult to separate from the discussion of sources above, in part because listening and reading extend metaphorically into a concatenation of sources, texts, landscapes, experiences and more. All of these led to the creation of this book.

My first and foremost acknowledgement is to the land on which I stand and upon which I write. I acknowledge the animal life, plant life and the elements that make up this place. These are lands of ongoing Indigenous presence in this place currently called Canada, and I acknowledge my relationship to the treaties that make it possible for me to be in this place. I strive – and then fail and then strive anew – to help this place become a better one for those who will come after me. I live and work in Treaty 7 territory. Treaty 7 was signed in 1877 between representatives of the Crown and local Indigenous nations. The nations are those of the Niitsitapi (Blackfoot) confederacy – Piikani, Siksika and Kainai; the Stoney Nakoda nations – Wesley, Chiniki and Bearspaw; and the Tsuut'ina Nation. The Métis Nation of Alberta, Region 3, also calls these lands home. The lands that make up the province of Alberta – and the lands about which I write – are also covered by Treaties 4 (1874), 6 (1876),

8 (1899) and 10 (1906). Many nations and people constitute this place. Its histories and present-day Indigenous resurgence deserve more space than I can give here. These deserve, rather, the full and thoughtful work that Indigenous writers, artists, historians, storytellers, communities and academics are dedicating to these subjects. In that spirit, and thinking of northern Alberta, I encourage readers to seek works by Driftpile Cree author Billy-Ray Belcourt and Wapsewsipi (Swan River) Cree author Dallas Hunt.

I acknowledge my colleagues at the University of Calgary and at Mount Royal University. Discussions with them made this book possible. Thank you to the Banff Centre for Arts and Creativity, and to derek beaulieu in particular, for supporting the residency in January 2020 that allowed me to begin to pull this manuscript together. Thank you to the University of Salamanca, Spain, and especially to Ana María Fraile-Marcos, for providing generous hospitality in February and March of 2020, just as the pandemic set in. I am sorry to my colleagues and friends in Spain that I was forced to return early to Canada due to the pandemic. I look forward to a time when we might meet again.

Noelle Allen at Wolsak and Wynn put her trust in this project when it was only an idea, and that trust has been important to me beyond measure. Tremendous thanks to her, to Ashley Hisson, whose keen editorial eye improved this work immeasurably, and to everyone at Wolsak and Wynn.

This book is a result of years of listening to stories told by family and friends, for which I am also thankful. It is my sincere hope that I have represented everyone well, with the respect and care due to people living their lives in sometimes difficult circumstances. The shortcomings, flaws and slippery memories represented in these pages should be attributed to me alone. I miss my granny, Kathleen Dobson, who shows up often here, but also everyone who has departed ahead of me. I think of Ken Dobson, John Gora, Darlene

Gora and more. Thank you to my parents and sister, as well as my grandmother, June Gora, for always being there and for being patient with me. During the editing of this book, poet and editor Doug Barbour and Stó:lō writer and public intellectual Lee Maracle both passed away, and I would like to note the profound impact that both, in very different ways, have had on my practice. Many people – friends, colleagues and writers; more than I am able to list here – also contributed their thoughts, ideas and support. Thank you all.

My children are a constant source of pride, as well as reminders of what is at stake in how we listen to the land. And, as ever, this book couldn't have happened without Aubrey Jean Hanson.

Kit Dobson lives and works in Calgary / Treaty 7 territory in southern Alberta. His previous books include *Malled: Deciphering Shopping in Canada* and he is a professor in the Department of English at the University of Calgary. He grew up in many places across Canada, but returned again and again to the landscapes of northern Alberta where his family members settled – and that continue to animate his thinking.